CW00972870

## The Social Market Foundatio

The Foundation's main activi
publish original papers by inc ~~p~~ ......... academic and other
experts on key topics in the economic and social fields, with
a view to stimulating public discussion on the performance of
markets and the social framework within which they operate.
The Foundation is a registered charity and a company limited
by guarantee. It is independent of any political party or group
and is financed by the sale of publications and by voluntary
donations from individuals, organisations and companies.
The views expressed in publications are those of the authors
and do not represent a corporate opinion of the Foundation.

## In association with acevo

acevo (Association of Chief Executives of Voluntary
Organisations) is the professional body representing charity
and not-for-profit sector chief executives in England and Wales,
with 2000 members. It aims to inspire effective leadership in
a modern, enterprising third sector. The sector now employs
the full-time equivalent of 1.5m staff, with a collective annual
turnover of £46bn.

Third Sector Leaders

First published by
The Social Market Foundation,
July 2005

The Social Market Foundation
11 Tufton Street
London SW1P 3QB

Designed by Paula Snell Design

# Contents

*"We can't solve problems by using the same kind of thinking we used when we created them."*

**Albert Einstein (1879-1955)**

# Foreword

This book contributes to an important and exciting debate about the future shape of public service delivery. We are all customers, so we all have a stake in the outcome. So too does the Government, which must not only secure significant improvements but also translate that progress into positive public perceptions of their achievement.

The third sector, encompassing the full range of Britain's not-for-profit organisations, has a significant reserve of public trust, "ground level" service delivery experience (as well as understanding the often severe impact of delivery failures) and the ability to engage with citizens at the individual level. So how does the Government best draw on those assets?

Working Links is a public/private joint venture company that delivers employment related services to many of the UK's most disadvantaged people and communities. In many ways we have a foot in all three camps, public, private and charitable (through the Links Foundation). We are delighted to endorse acevo's leadership of this debate on the role of the third sector: they are excellently qualified to fulfil that role. We may not sub-scribe to every view, analysis and conclusion presented, but this just serves to add value to the debate rather than detract from it.

In brief, our own belief is that the third sector is not an alternative to the private sector, it is a complementary partner that brings different skills, resources and objectives. Solutions should be based on recognising that the private sector often provides the most appropriate interface with Government in a contracting environment, although some of the largest charities can match this, but the third sector is an essential element in the supply chain that should have a defined role in the delivery specification, allowing even the smallest charities access to the market.

One of the most interesting ideas explored here involves joint ventures between private companies and not-for-profits. Collaborations between the two sectors remain in their infancy, but could represent an effective model for future delivery. At their best, they can combine private companies' effectiveness in negotiating and managing contracts with the third sector's ongoing commitment to service users' needs.

Welcome to the debate.

**Keith Faulkner CBE**
Managing Director
Working Links (Employment) Ltd

# Introduction

Public service reform in the UK is usually framed as a dramatic fight for the heart of the welfare state between the public and the private sector. The private sector is seen as embodying the virtues of efficiency, effective management skills and the potential for innovation while the public sector is seen as standing for public service ethos, high professional standards and good working practices. Where you stand on this battlefield is determined by the weight that you place on these various virtues.

However seductive, this view of public service reform is also reductive. It ignores the huge range of models for service provision in which public and private shade together in public private partnerships. It misses the existence of one whole sector altogether – one that is quietly getting on with the business of providing services, often to those most in need – the third sector. It also gives priority to structures when we should be most concerned with the interests of users. They are likely to care much more about the quality of service they receive than who provides it.

Our collective blindness to the virtues that recommend the third sector as a provider of public services is partly a product of the fire and fury of the reform debate. But it also has more deep-seated roots in the particular history of the welfare state in the UK. Philanthropy fell out of favour in the UK as universal state services came into being. It was seen as judgmental, partial and ad-hoc when, after the Second World War, access to healthcare, good schooling and support for the elderly and unemployed came to be seen as a right to be provided by the state.

The United States is often cited as the alternative model for welfare provision. In the US there has always been a

traditional role for charities in providing some of the funda-
mentals of support for those who are not able to work. Critics
argue that this has allowed the US government to get away
with a harsher, more minimal approach to welfare than those
found in European social democracies.

Over the last 50 years, the UK approach to the welfare
state has been much closer to this European model than to the
US model. Benefits are delivered as a right for all citizens and
it is the state's duty to provide. The role that this has left for
charities and other civil society organisations has been to pick
up where the state left off – in other words to provide services
at the margin, and where state support failed.

The current set of reforms are moving us away from this
European approach, but not in the direction of the United
States. We are not attempting to roll back the state in the way
that the neo-Liberals advocate, rather the opposite. Spending
on core public services has grown under Labour. Instead, the
government is recasting the state's role as a funder rather than
a deliverer of services.

This does not undermine the view that the state should
take responsibility for the provision of welfare in this country
since the state still funds services. What it does do is broaden
the way in which those services are delivered. So for charities
and other third sector organisations, their role can develop
beyond providing and funding services at the margins of the
welfare state, to providing (although not funding) core public
services.

So whether or not you believe in the provision of benefits
as a right or not, it is time to examine afresh what the voluntary
and charity sector can offer as a deliver of public services.
There are two very compelling reasons to regard third sector
organisations as important potential players in the reforming
public services.

The first is their ability to personalise services.
Personalisation – the provision of services in a way in which
users want to receive them, as opposed to the way service
providers want to deliver them – is the one thing that all sides
of the debate about reform agree on, albeit from different view-
points. Some argue from a consumerist perspective – that our
increasingly high expectations of services make personalisation

essential if public support for state funding is going to be maintained, particularly amongst the middle classes who have a choice about whether to go elsewhere. Others argue for personalisation because of serious concerns about the inequities which result from the current welfare systems. For example, articulate and well-informed patients are adept at getting the best from the NHS, while others are not. As a result, those most in need tend to get a poorer service. Personalisation would help address this by focusing more attention on the needs of each individual.

Personalisation is impossible without a number of different providers offering a range of services which are clearly differentiated. These must be differentiated on grounds which are important to the user of those services, rather than to service providers. This could be by location, by the way services are accessed, by the time they are available or by the very nature of the service itself.

Third sector organisations have a particularly important role here. As Nick Aldridge describes later in this book, most have evolved from the bottom up in response to the realisation of real need on the ground, rather than having been centrally planned as have most state services. This gives them both privileged understanding of the needs of those who use their services, but also a culture which tends to look down to the grassroots for a sense of direction, rather than up to central government.

The second major benefit the third sector brings is its close connection to the communities in which they work, which often involves not just providing services to local people, but also drawing their staff, including volunteers from those communities. This makes them part of the fabric of the local civil society. Giving charities a bigger role in direct service provision should also have the added benefit of building social capital and building a robust civil society – it should break down the barriers between "them"– those outsiders with power and control who intervene in communities, for good or ill - and "us" – those who have things done to them.

However there are some bear traps for both government and the third sector in growing the latter's role as providers of public services, and they relate closely to the two benefits I have described.

Taking on the role of provider of public service, funded by government, will bring third sector organisations within the scope of the government's evaluation and audit machine. There may be some scope, as Nick Aldridge suggests later in this paper, for a lighter touch, but thorough evaluation will still need to take place, particularly since it is the public's money that is being spent. It will take considerable expertise on the part of those running third sector organisations to retain a culture which gives primacy to the needs of those they serve, while meeting targets and quality thresholds set by government.

As I suggested above, one of the reasons we should value third sector organisations is because they are part of the fabric of civil society – neither state nor market. Their presence brings broad benefits to society as a whole through fostering a sense of community and engagement. It also brings specific benefits to service users, since voluntary sector organisations are often valued and trusted by service users precisely because they are not the state. It is vital that third sector organisations retain that clear distinction between themselves and the state on whose behalf they provide services.

So is the challenge for the government and for those third sector organisations who want to get involved in the provision of services – to grow into the role without losing what makes the third sector particularly valued as a service provider. This is a huge management challenge for third sector leaders, but also for government. It will need to develop monitoring techniques and funding mechanisms which foster rather than squash the characteristics that makes the third sector unique.

**Ann Rossiter**
Acting Director
Social Market Foundation

# Executive summary

This book sketches out a framework for putting communities and citizens in charge of public services. It highlights the potential of specialist third sector organisations[1] in reforming and delivering key tranches of the Government's programme, resulting in more user-focused, responsive public services. It outlines the barriers to such a programme, and proposes concrete measures to catalyse the process of reform.

The Labour Party's Manifesto aims to deliver, "services free to all, personal to each… and driving innovation through diversity of provision and power in the hands of the patient, the parent and the citizen." A key strand of the Government's programme of public service reform has been to open up public service markets to private companies and to the third sector, incorporating Britain's charities and not-for-profit organisations. Both the Conservatives and the Liberal Democrats have also highlighted the sector's potential contribution to public service reform and delivery.

The Labour Manifesto recognises that the third sector, incorporating Britain's charities and not-for-profit organisations, "has shown itself to be innovative, efficient and effective," and argues that "its potential for service delivery should be considered on equal terms." It goes on to outline the specific areas in which the third sector could make a particularly significant contribution: employment training, children's services, correctional services, health services and education.

The third sector plays a dual role in public service reform. First, it articulates the views and needs of the communities and citizens who benefit from public services, helping to inform service design and delivery. Second, where the third sector can drive up service quality through direct involvement, it has a significant and growing role in public service delivery. Some of the most widely respected third sector organisations, such as NACRO, RNID, and Turning Point, perform both roles, using the experience they have gained through substantial programmes of service delivery to inform their advocacy strategies.

The Government's intention to make the third sector an equal partner in public service reform has been widely articulated. However, this central commitment has not translated into the concrete reforms that would make such engagement a reality. This book revisits the general case for a greater third sector role in public service delivery, and seeks to move the debate forward by examining the case and prerequisites for a major expansion of third sector activity within four significant areas:

1 employment training services (Chapter 3)

2 children's services (Chapter 4)

3 independent living aids (Chapter 5)

4 correctional services (Chapter 6)

Together, they provide a compelling illustration of the third sector's potential, which extends across a far broader range of public services than this book is able to examine. In each of them:

- Government's policy aims align closely with the priorities and expertise of expert third sector organisations,
- statutory services have experienced difficulties in meeting those policy aims effectively and efficiently, and
- potential models to scale up the third sector's involvement are already being explored by third sector organisations and by government.

Building on the experience of successful independent providers of public services, within each area we suggest a range of measures that would enable the third sector to fulfil its full potential as a service provider. They include:

- conversion, through which assets are transferred from the public sector to independent organisations, providing the capacity and security to develop innovative services in the long-term,

- contestability, through which public service markets are opened to increased competition, driving up quality, efficiency and innovation, and
- joint ventures, which exemplify a long-term partnership approach conditional on shared goals and shared risks.

We recognise, however, that a number of significant barriers continue to restrict the third sector's role in public service delivery. Chief among these are:

- poor procurement practices, which result in contracts that are not fit for purpose,
- insecurity and instability in the funding environment, making it difficult for third sector organisations to access capital and invest in the development of services and staff,
- the bureaucratic nature of collaborative arrangements between third sector and government, discouraging organisations from taking on a greater role,
- the sector's lack of capacity and expertise, resulting from historic underinvestment in infrastructure and organisational development,
- the risk that the sector's approach to accountability and best practice in governance will fall short of that expected by public sector partners,
- the costs and risks inherent in developing new services that focus on the hardest-to-help groups.

We close by recommending four measures to build on this initial analysis, with a view to implementing reforms that would make the third sector a central partner in public service reform, to the advantage of taxpayers and service users:

1 A cross-governmental implementation team should be established to scope a framework for reform in more detail and make recommendations to the Cabinet Office within 18 months.

2 Within each of the market segments we have highlighted, further work should be undertaken to analyse the added value of third sector delivery, explore the practical potential for greater third sector involvement, and encourage the establishment of consortia to increase capacity.

3  Additional market segments should be explored in more detail, including:

- mental health and learning
- education in schools
- drug treatment
- social care and older people

4  More detailed monitoring of third sector involvement in public service delivery should be undertaken to provide a more reliable indicator of the success of governmen policy initiatives in driving forward third sector involvement.

# Chapter 1: Third time lucky? The third sector and public service reform

*The government wants a greater role for the third sector in public services*

The reform of public services is a crucial issue for all sections of society. The core challenge in the reform agenda is that services are currently designed by professionals and reflect institutional needs; the risk is that unless this changes, service users – communities and citizens – are left to fit in to the model. The debate must take the needs of communities and citizens, rather than those of providers and purchasers, as its starting point.

Third sector organisations have delivered public services, based on the needs of communities and citizens, for centuries. In many recent examples, our services have grown out of the frustration that citizens experience in accessing mainstream public services. Often they see services delivered that ignore or downplay the real needs of communities, and move to fill the gaps.

Many of the most powerful examples of third sector delivery, such as Coram Family's joined-up services for children, Motability's unique mobility services for disabled people, RNID's programme of audiology reform, or Turning Point's "connected care services", illustrate the growth of the third sector in response to the failure of statutory services to meet needs.

The Labour Party's General Election Manifesto states that the Government aims to "make public services safe for a generation," aspiring to deliver "services free to all, personal to each… and driving innovation through diversity of provision and power in the hands of the patient, the parent and the citizen."

A key strand of the Government's programme of public service reform has been to open up public service markets to a greater diversity of providers. The overarching objective of the 2004 Spending Review was to provide the public, through a major programme of investment, with high quality services tailored to the needs of individuals and communities.[2] The Government therefore wishes to encourage a greater say for public service users in shaping the services they receive. It sees the third sector as a natural partner, both in providing personalised services, and as an advocate for service users in the ongoing debate on public service reform.

The Manifesto states that the third sector - Britain's charities and not-for-profit organisations - "has shown itself to be innovative, efficient and effective," and argues that "its potential for service delivery should be considered on equal terms." Both the Conservatives and Liberal Democrats have also drawn attention to the third sector's potential as a service provider, and argued broadly for measures that would help the sector fulfil it.[3]

Communities must be put back in charge of the services they receive, and citizens must play a central role in public service reform. Who better to facilitate this role than the many thousands of third sector organisations that advocate for service reform on their behalf?

### Service delivery and the third sector agenda

In January 2001, Gordon Brown wrote an article about the third sector's power, referring to its credibility and established presence in communities. He said that over the next five years we would see "The biggest transformation in the relationship between the state and voluntary action for a century."[4]

The third sector plays a dual role in public service reform. At its best, the sector articulates the views and needs of the communities and citizens who receive public services, helping to inform service design and delivery through powerful advocacy. Second, where the sector has specialist expertise or strong community links, it can also drive up service quality through direct involvement in delivery.

Some of the most widely respected third sector organisations perform both roles, using the experience they have gained

through substantial programmes of service delivery to inform
their advocacy strategies. For example, RNID, the largest
charity for deaf and hard of hearing people, ran a vigorous
campaign to improve the quality of hearing aid provision while
taking on a growing role in audiology procurement in collaboration with the NHS. NACRO, the crime reduction charity,
works directly with 60,000 ex-offenders every year, while
campaigning to shape policies that reduce offending.

The third sector's public service agenda must have one
overriding aim: to improve public services for the good of
citizens and communities. Third sector organisations do not
primarily seek expansion for its own sake, or to secure
increased financial gain. They are mission-driven and not-for-
profit. Their mission is to drive up quality, ensuring that
services are high-quality, professionally delivered, and focused
closely on users' needs. In general, third sector organisations
aspire to take on public service delivery when, and only when,
they believe that they can run the service more effectively than
the state.[5]

Britain's third sector is already delivering high quality,
innovative and personalised services to hard-to-reach clients,
notably in the fields of housing and social care. Yet its immense
potential as a key partner in public service delivery remains
largely unfulfilled. Despite growing political focus on the
sector's role in shaping and delivering key services, it is still highly
specialised and marginal.

A recent indicative sample of acevo's 2000 Chief
Executives[6] suggested that just over half run organisations
primarily engaged in service delivery, while around one fifth are
campaigning and advocacy organisations. The remainder are
grant-makers and associations, working to build the sector's
capacity and professionalism across the full range of its activities.

*The third sector's public service agenda
must have one overriding aim: to
improve public services for the good
of citizens and communities.*

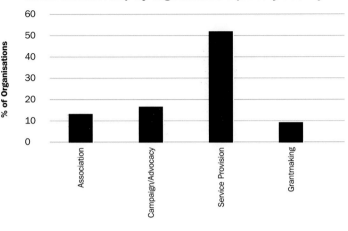

**acevo membership by organisation's primary activity**

Some commentators have raised concerns that the charitable purpose of organisations might be diluted or distorted by a greater focus on public service delivery. In many ways, the distinction is artificial: many long-established charities have delivered public services for centuries. For example, the first "children's centre" was established in 1739 by Coram Family[7]. Other leading charities, such as Turning Point or NCH, already receive all or most of their funding from public service delivery contracts.

Although many third sector organisations have a flexible and enterprising approach to service development, they also tend to be strongly focused on their missions. There is no suggestion that organisations should deliver services that run counter to those missions, or that campaigning or capacity building organisations should be encouraged by government to engage more directly in service delivery.

Indeed, the vital role of non-service providing organisations should be better recognised and encouraged by government. Third sector organisations play a major role in ensuring that the experience of citizens and service users informs the government's programme, both directly, through advocacy and indirectly through its work to strengthen the networks that constitute civil society. Commentators have pointed to a risk that through the ongoing focus on public service reform, "the civil society aspect of debates about the sector can be lost".[8]

This aspect of the sector's work deserves more emphasis. As the National Council for Voluntary Organisations (NCVO), puts it:

"Government needs to develop a better understanding of the important role Voluntary and Community Organisations play campaigning or advocating on behalf of service users, communities or individuals and how this contributes to achieving better public services."[9]

Moreover, for those third sector organisations that do want to play a greater role in public service delivery, the process through which change occurs is fundamental. Too rapid an expansion or transfer of responsibility risks reconstituting third sector organisations in the image of public sector agencies. Such an eventuality would undermine the rationale for involving the third sector at all. Instead, major reforms should be planned properly, enabling organisations within all the sectors to decide where and how they can contribute. For this reason, third sector organisations must be involved in setting the terms of trade for the service delivery they take on. Only through such involvement will they guarantee that service delivery will help them to achieve their missions on a sustainable basis.

The current political agenda provides an unprecedented opportunity for many third sector organisations to become more equal partners for the government in public service reform. A change in the terms of trade would enable those organisations to achieve better results for the people they exist to serve. While both sides have demonstrated the will to build closer engagement, the potential of this engagement has not yet been realised. This paper is intended to encourage further steps towards fulfilling that potential.

## Improving service quality through third sector involvement

Considerable research has been undertaken into the "added value" offered by the third sector, understood as generic benefits that tend to characterize delivery by third sector organisations. These studies[10] have suggested that the third sector's advantages may result in providers delivering a higher quality of service, at a better price, than their counterparts from the other sectors. These potential advantages include:

## User-focus

Third sector organisations are mission-driven, rather than aiming primarily for profits. They therefore have relatively little incentive to compromise on service quality in order to increase margins or meet competing priorities. However, all third sector organisations must remain sustainable, and should therefore seek to generate small surpluses for reinvestment in their activities. Acevo has encouraged the sector to calculate its cost base accurately, enabling negotiation from a more informed position. Thus financial pressures motivate third sector organisations to maximize efficiency, while their mission-led approach implies maintaining the quality of the services above all else.

This ongoing, mission-driven commitment to the needs of particular groups of service users can make the third sector an attractive partner for government in developing long-term service strategies. This commitment to the needs of service users becomes particularly valuable in developing services where public funders experience difficulties in monitoring performance, perhaps because of problems in defining and measuring concrete outcomes. In addition, the third sector, particularly in comparison with the public sector, is relatively resistant to domination by professional interests. Excessive professional control over public institutions "can put the brake on decisive and timely action at a local level".[11]

## Flexibility, innovation and joining up

Third sector providers are able to work across government silos, joining up funding streams and policies. The starting point for many organisations is the service users' needs, rather than the funder's contract specifications. They have therefore become expert in resourcing innovative packages of services around people's multiple needs, often channelling multiple funding streams from government to provide a complete service.

If delivered by government, services would frequently remain fragmented and hard to access, reflecting the separation between individual policy responsibilities and funding streams.

In contrast, the third sector's autonomy and relative independence from the policy-making process enables a more dynamic and less bureaucratic[12] approach to service delivery.

---

**Vista: responsive services for visually impaired people**

Vista provides the majority of services for visually impaired people in Leicestershire, Leicester and Rutland. It has service level agreements to provide statutory services on behalf of the Social Service Departments in those authorities.

Vista contacts users within 5 days of their registration as blind or partially sighted; and makes the first visit within 28 days of receiving the form. In neighbouring counties and the rest of the United Kingdom, especially some London Boroughs, it can take between 6 months and a year for that visit to occur.

Vista runs an integrated service in its Resources Centre. A low vision clinic is funded by the NHS Trusts. When a piece of equipment is recommended for a person, they can walk 10 yards across the building and usually receive it immediately from their Resource Area, funded under service level agreement by the local authorities.

The chief executive, Gordon Diffey, says: "What we have tried to do, but I honestly believe we can still do better, is to have as near an integrated process as our funders will allow."[13]

---

**Social capital**

In addition to their close focus on service users, third sector providers often bring together professional staff and volunteers to accomplish their goals. Since high quality service providers invest heavily in training and managing their volunteers, public participation in service delivery through volunteering helps to build individuals' skills. By involving members of the community in delivery, volunteering increases community engagement with, and ownership of, public services.

Volunteers' presence and input can also drive up service quality, and diversify the third sector workforce. This general characteristic fosters active citizenship and community empowerment, and contributes towards the delivery of the

Government's civil renewal agenda. Such activity, however, is rarely funded by statutory purchasers as part of service delivery, despite the wider benefits it brings to local communities.

---

**SeeAbility: Seeing value in the third sector**
By David Scott-Ralphs, Chief Executive
"SeeAbility (formerly the Royal School for the Blind), is a charity that works with people who have a sight impairment combined with learning and other additional disabilities. The charity has over 200 years of experience in providing residential support, day activity and specialist rehabilitation services. Whilst originally funded through philanthropy, its main funding sources in the modern era have been local authorities and health trusts.

Service users are referred to SeeAbility mainly through statutory agencies, which are often in search of an urgent solution for an individual with complex disabilities whose previous placement has broken down. A significant number of people with learning disabilities, autism and degenerative illnesses have a severe sight impairment which is often not properly diagnosed or dealt with. The result can be pain and discomfort, leading to behaviour that challenges those providing support. Such individuals are often shunted around the system, being placed in totally inappropriate settings or high cost emergency respite services. SeeAbility's specialism means that the total needs of people with these complex disabilities can be met, providing a cost-effective and long-term solution for statutory agencies.

As a charity, SeeAbility is able to engage more effectively with families and with the local community than a statutory agency ever could. It has been very successful in recruiting volunteers to add value to its core support service, from befriending through to driving, IT support and even tandem cycling. At its Leatherhead operation alone, around 80 volunteers provide some 500 hours of support a month, at an annual value of £50,000. Whilst SeeAbility expects and receives full cost recovery for its support services, the extended networks that it has managed to create around its projects provide additional funding for 'quality of life' extras, such as sensory gardens (often created by corporate supporters) and new equipment, to the tune of around £500,000 a year."[14]

## Local accountability

Localism has become a key part of the political agenda, with all the major parties agreeing that local autonomy can increase the quality and responsiveness of local services. A framework of national standards must be complemented by a degree of local control over service design. Third sector organisations are better placed to resist excessive central control over service design than bodies that operate within the public sector, and therefore to develop bespoke services in response to local needs.

The third sector, like government, consists of national, regional and local organisations. Attention must be given to the best geographical basis on which to deliver services. As a guiding principle, services currently provided by central government departments might best be transferred to consortia of national organisations. Services currently delivered by local authorities, particularly those where community ownership is of central importance, might best be transferred to local or regional organisations.

However, there may also be an opportunity for further devolution in some areas of delivery, bringing currently centralised services, such as employment and correctional services, down to a more regional or local level through new delivery mechanisms.

The ODPM has unveiled a range of measures aimed at putting power into the hands of local communities. Over a quarter of local authorities have already established structures that have given decision-making powers to communities. ODPM proposes a Charter to set out what local people should expect from services, and in terms of control or influence over their neighbourhoods. Some parts of the Charter would be universal, and others would be decided locally. They might include:

- establishing "triggers" for local communities to require action where they are dissatisfied with a particular service,
- devolving budgets and giving communities the power to manage particular services directly,
- giving communities ownership of local assets like play grounds and community centres, and the chance to manage them themselves.[15]

Building on the Sustainable Communities agenda, devolution to third sector, community-based ownership could depend on certain "triggers". Where local communities are dissatisfied with a particular service, they could demand changes, such as the chance to manage particular services directly by devolving budgets to community level.

Strong, vocal communities are a precondition for such devolution, and for the localism agenda in general. From this perspective, they are a key component of the Government's programme of public service reform. Julia Unwin and Peter Molyneux note that, "service delivery alone is not enough. Without the development of strong, resilient and empowered communities, the intention of delivering better services will always be frustrated".[16]

In some market segments, a combination of national and local delivery may be appropriate. For example, local childcare services are likely to benefit from local ownership, while a parenting helpline would be delivered most cost-effectively by national organisations. These considerations should be paramount in fostering new markets for third sector service delivery.

**Emphasis on social inclusion**
Much third sector expertise relates to the hardest to help groups, who are often those with significant multiple needs. Government research has repeatedly demonstrated that the most socially excluded groups in society suffer from multiple dimensions of disadvantage. For example, in accessing health services older people suffer from a paucity of social networks as well as limited contact with mainstream providers.[17]

Socially excluded people often require a "joined-up" service, including assistance in liasing with the relevant government departments and agencies. Many community organisations exist to articulate these needs from the user's point of view, ensuring that the voice of hard-to-reach groups is heard in service planning and development.

The independence of third sector organisations from governmental control, and the links they have made through local advocacy, mean they are often more trusted by service users, particularly among those who are socially excluded, or who have lost faith in statutory services. Trust in the charitable sector, for example, remains far higher than in the majority of public or private sector institutions.[18] This can enable third sector organisations to engage with people who might otherwise be excluded from service provision.

In many such areas the state does not yet deliver a tailored service, and there remains little understanding of the likely cost of provision. Yet the potential long-term benefits of such services to society, and resulting savings to the public purse, demand further exploration. The New Economics Foundation's research into the concept of Social Return on Investment represents a significant step forward in quantifying the long-term economic return on social interventions.[19] Leonard Cheshire's service for the most demanding learning-disabled children provides a powerful illustration of the benefits and challenges involved in developing such services.

---

**Leonard Cheshire: an innovative partnership for high-risk services**

Hollow Lane, a specialist Leonard Cheshire service in Exeter, was developed from a partnership between Education, Health and Social Services which had collectively identified a need for residential provision for the most demanding learning-disabled children in the Exeter and wider Devon area.

A range of children had been identified who were living a long way from home and family, or in inappropriate accommodation, resulting in spiralling staff injuries due to lack of specialist staff and training. The partners considered options including greater use of out-of-county placements (normally privately owned and high cost) but concluded that a small, properly staffed, local residential service near a specialist school was the 'best value' solution.

Leonard Cheshire was one of the few providers willing to take on such a 'high-risk' service and gave a price within the tendering process for a given level of staffing. Before proceeding the following methodology was developed:

• Leonard Cheshire would provide an open book approach to

---

budgeting, showing how all costs were made up in as much detail as was wanted;

- A partnership monitoring group would be set up to include representation from Health, Social Services, Education and Leonard Cheshire. This group would make a recommendation for an annual increase based on increasing/decreasing needs of the children. The contract states "In the event that the staffing levels fail to meet the requirements...the service purchaser agrees to amend the contract price" and "The purchaser will be required to agree this recommended price increase unless it has reasonable grounds for believing that costs are increasing at a lower rate". In practice, during the first year of operation, the price has increased twice and this has been agreed;
- A risk schedule was developed. This states that the capital risk for the building cost would fall to Leonard Cheshire, but that the revenue risk of operating the service would fall to the commissioners.

On this basis Leonard Cheshire found a site, built a specialist residential service, and recruited and trained staff. The service has now been open and running successfully for over a year. This very risk prone service, with a large number of cost variables, continues to flourish on the basis of this mature open contracting basis. The acute nature of the need being met helps to ensure that all parties remain focused and working in partnership.[20]

Expanding such services on a larger scale would require significant initial investment and political commitment to long-term benefits, both of which are becoming increasingly evident. ODPM's Sustainable Communities Plan announces an intention to "Focus on the disadvantaged and champion them as services are transformed across government," by "using the experiences of the bottom 10% as a litmus test of reform across government".[21]

## Specific areas for reform

While the Government, through HM Treasury and the Home Office, has invested considerable resources in the sector as a whole, its attention is now moving to the contribution the sector can make to particular targets and policy priorities. The £125m Futurebuilders Investment Fund, launched in 2004, was established specifically to fund organisations delivering services in the fields of community cohesion and crime, education and learning, health and social care, and support for children and young people.

The Labour Manifesto briefly highlights specific areas where greater third sector involvement would improve delivery, including employment training, children's services, offenders' services and health. It states, for example, that Labour will "welcome new independent and voluntary sector partners to provide job-seeking services," and that "Voluntary organisations and the private sector will be offered greater opportunities to deliver offender services."

This book seeks to move the debate forwards by providing an initial analysis of high potential services within each of these four areas. Both the Government and the third sector agree that greater collaboration would, in principle, improve the quality and responsive of public services. The challenge for both is to ensure that, within these areas, the transformation they envisage now takes place.

# Chapter 2: Driving change

This report provides an initial analysis of several areas of public service delivery with the potential for dramatically increased third sector involvement. Within each area the majority of service delivery is currently undertaken directly by the public sector, including local government, primary care trusts and government agencies. It suggests actions by the government that would enable the third sector to take on a much greater role in designing and delivering those services, with the potential to benefit service users.

We propose three models through which a dramatically increased third sector role could develop: conversion, contestability and joint ventures. Within each of the areas, we make proposals for a more central third sector role, building on some or all of these models of delivery.

## Conversion

Under a conversion model, responsibilities and key assets are directly transferred from the public sector to the third sector, by:

a) **reconstituting** public sector organisations as independent, third sector organisations, or by

b) **transferring** assets from the public sector to existing third sector organisations.

### Case study: housing associations

Housing associations[22] provide an example of dramatically expanded public service delivery through the third sector. In 1974 housing associations managed only 100,000 homes in the UK; they now manage over 1.8 million – holding an asset base of £60 billion, and continuing to expand. Since the late

1980s almost all new social housing has been provided by
housing associations. ODPM envisages continuing growth in its
five year plan.[23]

There is evidence that housing associations add value to
service delivery, resulting in increased tenant satisfaction. The
Joseph Rowntree Foundation reports that "housing management
performance (and average tenant satisfaction) tends to improve
following stock transfer." Although there is no clear evidence
that housing associations outperform comparable local
authorities, "they set standards which others struggle to match."[24]

## Capital investment and asset bases

The housing sector was exceptional in the vast asset base
it had developed before 1988, as a result of its access to
public funds. This asset base provided associations with
sufficient collateral to support access to loans, providing
a stable basis for expansion.

Housing associations benefited from upfront capital
grants for new development, combined with a relatively
secure stream of funding from housing benefit. These factors
encouraged them to use the opportunities presented for
accessing private sector capital, from which they receive
over £25 billion per year.

## Managed risks

The growth of housing associations from 1988 relied on the
fact that the funding regime placed only a limited, manageable,
burden of risk on the sector. Funders showed a willingness to
share risks, encouraged by the demonstrable successes of
housing associations in repaying loans, and by the presence
of a strong Housing Corporation as a funder and regulator.

For example, the use of varying proportions of grant
finance, dependent on the area of need (e.g. housing for key
workers), was a conscious effort at sharing variable risks
between funder and provider.

Housing associations illustrate the potential of capital
investment and efficient allocation of risk in contracts. It shows
the scale of potential implications for capacity building within
the third sector, joint ventures with the private sector, and the
expansion of service delivery that results.[25]

**Case study: leisure trusts**

The growth of leisure trusts, through which local authorities transfer assets to third sector organisations, provides another illustration of the phenomenon. A recent decision by the Charity Commission has made it clear that charities can be set up to deliver public services which public authorities have a statutory duty to provide, such as libraries.[26]

---

**Greenwich Leisure**

Greenwich Leisure Limited (GLL) is an innovative staff-led 'Leisure Trust', structured as an Industrial and Provident Society. It manages more than forty public leisure centres within the M25 area, in partnership with local authorities and other local government agencies.

GLL reinvests all its surpluses back into the service and facilities for the benefit of its customers and communities, with a view to supporting a stronger, sustainable, socially inclusive local economy.

The Trust won "Social Enterprise of the Year" Award at the National Business Awards 2004. Its Leisure Centres in the London Borough of Greenwich have been certified at the Charter Mark Standard, in recognition of its approach to customer service.[27]

---

# Contestability

Contestability involves the opening up of public service markets to new entrants, enabling third sector providers to compete for a larger market share.

Although the third sector remains a relatively small competitor in the public services market, some organisations have become service providers of significant scale by winning statutory contracts for delivery.

**Case study: Turning Point**

In its 40 years, Turning Point has grown from a single alcohol project in South East London to become the UK's leading independent social care organisation, working in the areas of substance misuse, mental health and learning disability.

It aims to provide "connected care", focusing on people

rather than individual problems. By sharing learning across different areas of provision, it can provide joined-up services to meet a wide range of needs:

- supported housing for people with mental health problems and with a learning disability,
- drug and alcohol services including advice and education for young people, rehabilitation services, counselling, outreach work, and support services for friends and family members,
- outreach services for people with mental health problems including emergency helplines, support for carers and support for people living independently in their own homes,
- education and employment programmes such as the Government-backed Progress2work scheme,
- support services across these areas in prisons and working with probation and youth offender services.

Turning Point is primarily a provider of public services, and now earns 98% of its income from contracts with local authorities and NHS commissioners. It runs support services in around 200 locations across England and Wales, helping 100,000 people each year. Turning Point sees immense potential for expansion in its range of services, given a more stable contractual relationship with the state.

### Case Study: Motability

Motability, a unique charity, changes the lives of disabled people who are unable or virtually unable to walk. Those who cannot afford a car or powered wheelchair, and would otherwise be housebound, can get one through the Motability scheme.

In 1976, the Government introduced a universal cash mobility allowance to replace a limited "vehicle scheme" for drivers only. The formation of Motability was announced in 1977, the result of the Government's belief that the best way to increase disabled people's mobility would be found outside government.

Its founders established a leasing scheme on preferential terms, which, for the first time, would bring cars within the reach of most people with the mobility allowance. Charitable funds would subsidise those for whom the allowance was insufficient to buy the car they needed.

Over 1.5 million disabled people in the UK currently qualify for the Higher Rate Mobility Component of Disability Living Allowance from the Government. What a disabled person chooses to do with that money is entirely up to them. Currently, 400,000 disabled people have chosen to have their allowances paid to the Scheme to meet the cost of having a car, powered wheelchair or scooter through a contract hire or hire purchase arrangement.

The scheme focuses on users' needs by bringing together a number of key partners:

- The Government (Department for Work and Pensions),
- Motability (the registered charity empowered by its Royal Charter),
- Motability Operations (owned by the UK's largest banks), operating the car schemes on a not-for-profit basis,
- route2mobility Ltd ("r2m"), a privately owned company which operates the powered wheelchair and scooter scheme,
- manufacturers of cars, powered wheelchairs and scooters,
- car dealers and dealers in powered wheelchairs and scooters,
- specialist vehicle adaptation companies,
- insurance and roadside assistance providers.

Cars are supplied new from Motability accredited dealerships and customers can choose from over 20 car brands. There are more than 3,500 Motability accredited car dealerships across the UK and a national network of accredited retailers of powered wheelchairs and scooters. The Motability scheme also provides a small number of used cars through hire purchase.

## Joint ventures

Joint ventures are vehicles for partners to share investment in, and ownership of, a new custom-built service provider. They thus provide a concrete illustration of the shared commitments that characterise partnership working at its best. They engender a culture of compromise and investment for the sake of mutual goals. This compares very favourably with the short-term and insecure nature of most contracts between third sector organisations and government.[28]

**Case study: Working Links**

Working Links is a public/private partnership (PPP), set up in 2000 to deliver the Government's Employment Zones[29] in some of Britain's most disadvantaged communities. Structured as a joint venture, owned partly by two private companies[30] and partly by government, it currently runs over 60 contracts on behalf of government agencies, including the Department for Work and Pensions and the Learning and Skills Council. It has placed over 40,000 long-term unemployed into jobs, including some of the hardest to help groups such as the long-term unemployed. With a turnover of £50m, it currently holds a significant proportion of the Welfare to Work market.

Working Links collaborates closely with partners from the public, private and third sectors, including specialist employment charities. Its primary role is as a facilitator, managing risks, building capacity and developing programmes to deliver results. Its added value comes through its ability to negotiate and manage contracts effectively with commissioners, and to develop capacity in its providers.

**Incentives and innovation**

Under the Employment Zones initiative, funding is related directly to outcomes. Providers make a surplus if they move clients into a sustainable job; otherwise they make a loss. This transfer of output risk was combined with the genuine intention to foster innovation: had they followed the public sector's usual practice, providers would not achieve the required improvement in performance.

Instead, consultants focus on each jobseeker's individual needs, identifying the most suitable jobs and helping them overcome whatever practical barriers they face in getting back to work. This can mean almost anything from arranging training or driving lessons, to paying for transport, childcare, or even new clothes for an interview. Once they find employment, the jobseeker's consultant provides ongoing support to both the jobseeker and employer, to ensure the job is sustainable.

**Features of the model**

By structuring Working Links as a joint venture, public and private sectors took on a genuine operational risk in its ongoing performance. Each partner provided a director of the joint venture, providing the organisation with vital operational skills and external credibility.

This shared ownership has a number of advantages. It has provided a space for a direct collaborative dialogue between public and private sector partners. By giving government a direct stake in the operation's success, it has encouraged monitoring and evaluation regimes to focus more closely on success, rather than the bureaucratic accountability and audit trails that characterise contractual relationships. It has helped Working Links to develop an internal culture that combines a public service ethos with private sector freedoms and disciplines.

Partners in any joint venture must identify, recognise, and manage the conflicts of interest involved. Working Links' governance requires unanimity: no two partners can overrule the third. As a result, owners' individual agendas are regularly reviewed and reconciled with that of the joint venture. A review in 2004 sought to ensure that its public sector ownership is distanced from the operational responsibilities of its public sector delivery partners.

**Lessons from the case studies**
The Government's current strategies for public service reform include:

- setting clear national standards in public services, bolstered by increased investment,
- driving innovation and personalisation by encouraging greater diversity of provision,
- increasing flexibility for local providers by removing red-tape and devolving responsibility, allowing them to respond to customer aspirations,
- placing greater power in the hands of service users, providing greater user choice in service provision.[31]

We believe that each of these models will contribute towards the government's reform agenda. The case studies given above illustrate the ways in which our models have improved service delivery, and suggest how these measures could be replicated or adapted in the future.

## Conversion: social housing

The social housing sector provides an instructive example of how capital investment and asset transfer can lead to a dramatic expansion in third sector service delivery. The organisational reforms that follow provide an opportunity to realign organisations with the priorities of their clients, and design innovative services more focused on users' needs. Placing assets at arm's length from the state can increase the capacity and freedom of providers, allowing them to show greater flexibility in responding to their users.

Such an expansion could be replicated where service delivery requires considerable capital assets, and a secure funding stream from service charges is assured. Prerequisites would include:

- the security of a fixed asset base for the third sector, generated through asset transfer or upfront capital grants,
- a commitment by public sector investors to share the risks inherent in such capital investment,
- a relatively secure revenue stream for providers, dependent on their delivery of services,
- a clear political will to drive through change.

## Contestability: Turning Point and Motability

In general, a more mixed economy of provision can drive up competition, improve service quality and deliver cost savings, as well as encouraging organisations to develop unique selling points through innovation and user involvement. Economic models suggest that increasing contestability in public service delivery tends to drive down prices while improving quality.[32]

Both Turning Point and Motability grew up in response to areas of identified need where statutory services were unable to provide a sufficiently user-focused solution. Although it is difficult to generalise widely from unique organisational stories, the following common factors have contributed to the success of each organisation within their chosen area:

- a highly developed and specialised offering which provides a sound basis for commercial competition,
- a strong conviction that the services they provide are,

or should be, mainstream services financed by the state,
- the expertise in commercial negotiations to win business on viable terms from statutory commissioners,
- the ability to join up a diverse range of funding sources and providers (or types of service) to create a single, coordinated, user-focused service.

### Joint ventures: Working Links

Joint ventures provide a mechanism for partnership working that makes explicit the shared interest all partners have in achieving the desired outcomes. Jointly owned vehicles can develop a workable degree of autonomy from each owner, while protecting and balancing the interests of each against those of the others.

Recent work by the Institute for Public Policy Research has recognised these benefits, while also noting the complex accountability mechanisms that can result:

"Joint ventures benefit from not relying on arm's length relationships between the public and private sectors – the organisational form of joint ventures gives tangible expression to the commitment to work in partnership. However, they can prove unstable in the face of changing circumstances and also raise difficult issues concerning accountability and risk transfer."[33]

Working Links demonstrates how a genuinely collaborative approach between commissioners and providers, through a joint venture, can result in outcome-focused service delivery on a large scale. The approach has enabled Working Links to negotiate towards a contracting regime that reflects acevo's Surer Funding Framework[34]:

1  risk is shared between partners,

2  contracts are of a sensible timescale,

3  bureaucracy is minimised,

4  pricing is fair, and related to performance.

Prerequisites for replicating such an expansion include:

- leadership and a genuine desire for innovation at senior level in the partner organisations,
- potential for a market scenario, combined with the political will to create it,
- presence in the joint venture of significant expertise in negotiating and managing contracts.

In the case of Working Links, private companies provided much of the joint venture's commercial expertise, providing valuable knowledge of contract negotiation and performance management. Within any similar partnership, work targeted at hard-to-reach groups would need to be subsidised through higher-margin, more mainstream work. Contracts will need to be structured in a way that ensures that this is prioritised by all members of the partnership.

# Chapter 3: Employment

## The market segment

Budget and policy responsibility
The budget and policy responsibility for ensuring employment opportunities are available to all lies primarily with the Department of Work & Pensions (DWP). A large part of DWP's efforts are concentrated through Jobcentre Plus.

In addition, various strands of this work lie with other departments, including:

(a) Department for Education & Skills (DfES):
• tackling the adult skills gap,
• ensuring 19 year olds are ready for skilled employment.

(b) HM Treasury:
• expand employment opportunities for all.

(c) Office of the Deputy Prime Minister:
• regional development and regeneration.

(d) The Home Office:
• employment training for offenders.

Current provision, including third sector role
Jobcentre Plus, an agency of DWP, currently undertakes the majority of provision. Its key objectives are to:

• increase the effective supply of labour by promoting work as the best form of welfare and helping unemployed and economically inactive people move into employment,
• work towards parity of outcomes for customers from minority ethnic groups,

- provide high-quality and demand-led services to employers, which help fill job vacancies quickly and effectively with well-prepared and motivated employees,
- help people facing the greatest barriers to employment to compete effectively in the labour market and move into and remain in work,
- improve continuously the quality, accessibility and delivery of services to all customers.

Jobcentre Plus also provides the benefits assessment service for the DWP. Its objectives under this heading are to:

- ensure that people receiving working-age benefits fulfil their responsibilities while providing appropriate help and support for those without work,
- pay customers the correct benefit at the right time and protect the benefit system from fraud, error and abuse.

The third sector contains a significant number of effective employment organisations, many of who specialise in reaching hard to help people:

---

**Shaw Trust** is the largest provider of employment services for disabled people and one of the largest providers of work focused alternatives to health and social services day care. It has over 60 contracts with Local Authorities and Health Trusts and currently provides one third of the Job Brokering service under New Deal for Disabled People, for Jobcentre Plus. In addition, it is the second largest provider of Workstep, still the government's main employment programme for disabled people.

---

**Tomorrow's People** is a specialist charitable trust, helping people out of long-term unemployment, welfare dependence or homelessness into jobs and self-sufficiency. It acts as an expert intermediary between government, business and individuals, using professional, dedicated staff to help the hardest to reach groups in their own communities. During the last twenty years, Tomorrow's People has helped 382,000 people in their quest to move out of long-term unemployment.

---

Scale/value of segment

The total operating cost of Jobcentre Plus, including administration and programmes, was £4.1 billion in 2003/04. There is additional spend, within the DWP budget, on people of working age. Spending from DfES over the same period on adult training/skills and lifelong-learning stood at £511 million. The DWP currently employs roughly 120,000 staff, of whom 84,000 work within Jobcentre Plus.

### The case for change
Impact and efficiency of current provision

Unemployment is at a 30-year low. According to the Office for National Statistics, the number of those seeking Jobseeker's Allowance stood at 839,400 in April 2005, representing a considerable success for the government. The unemployment rate is 2.6%, the lowest since the mid 1970s.

Contrastingly, the number of people claiming incapacity benefit has observed a very strong upward trend, now standing at 2.7 million. David Blunkett MP, the incoming Work and Pensions Secretary, is focusing closely on this issue. The Government aims to get up to one million incapacity benefit claimants back into work.[35]

Worklessness, which includes those on Jobseeker's Allowance and the economically inactive, is heavily concentrated in individual districts and wards. In the worst 1% of streets, more than half of all adults are out of work and on benefits. In some places, almost everyone is out of work and on benefits.

There is strong evidence that living in an area of concentrated worklessness damages the life chances of children and young people.[36] In particular, it lowers their expectations of employment, their chances of finding employment, and their chances of leaving poverty.

Many people living in areas of concentrated worklessness have:

- **multiple disadvantages**, such as disability and substance misuse,
- **low aspirations** for work, study and travel,
- **two or three generations out of work** in their family.

They are also likely belong to groups that pose particular challenges:

- **unqualified**: 50% of the working-age population in concentrations of worklessness have no qualifications,
- **black**: black people are more than twice as likely to live in these areas than the population as a whole,
- **limited by illness**: half of all households in these areas have at least one person with a limiting long-term illness,
- **full-time carers**: one third of carers in concentrations of worklessness provide more than 50 hours of unpaid care each week.[37]

Anecdotal evidence suggests that statutory services fail to provide for the hardest to help groups. Jobcentre Plus is, in general, unable to provide the level of training and after-placement support required by the long-term workless. The Social Exclusion Unit (SEU) has stated that, "Concentrations of worklessness have largely been missed by the activity to achieve the [DWP] target on disadvantaged areas, but changes to the way this target is devised will improve this".[38]

ODPM has specifically highlighted the "many people with disabilities who, with the right reasonable adjustments in the workplace, and the right attitude from employers, could make an important contribution to our economy".[39] According to the Shaw Trust, only 50% of disabled people of working age are currently in employment. Almost one million disabled people are economically inactive but would like to work.[40]

New efforts to reach the workless include the "New Deal for Skills" package, aimed at providing better support for those moving from welfare to work. It is focused on skills, and includes a one-to-one skills coaching service. The average cost per job, as calculated by the National Audit Office, stands at £3,500 for the New Deal and £3,700 for Employment Zones.

The illustrative case studies below show that the leading third sector organisations can achieve excellent results at impressive value for money. They focus intensively on building the soft skills and networks of their clients, an essential component in moving people from welfare to work. Many have particular expertise with individual groups: for instance, the Shaw

Trust works with employers and social services to help people with disabilities find employment, while the Black Training and Enterprise Group was established in 1991 to contribute to the economic revitalisation of black communities, supporting and mainstreaming the work of its practitioner members.

---

**LEAP** started in July 1993 as a black led project to help people from the former Harlesden City Challenge (HCC) area to find employment. So far, it has successfully filled around 3,000 vacancies.

In 1999 LEAP launched a major initiative, STRIVE, adapted from an American model, becoming the first organisation in Europe to do so. This innovative scheme is an empowerment programme that uses employment as the vehicle, and helps to change some of the underlying personal reasons why people cannot find and keep work.

Of Strive's client group:

- The majority of participants (79%) were of African and African Caribbean origin, there were slightly more female than male participants, and 30% were local residents,
- 59% of participants had been in receipt of state benefits with a third receiving Jobseeker's Allowance and one in ten receiving lone parent benefits.

An independent evaluation of Strive's work recently found that:

- nearly three quarters of Strive graduates were in paid work at the time they were surveyed, and another 6% had chosen to enter further training,
- just over 90% of those surveyed had had at least some paid work since graduating, and less than 5% of graduates had remained unemployed and actively seeking a job.[41]

---

### Devolution and community ownership

Employment services are vital in helping individuals to achieve their aspirations and potential, thus enabling their contribution to a healthy economy and reducing long-term dependency on the state. Employment services that can reach out to people, understand their issues on a personal consultancy basis, and provide long-term support to individuals (ensuring the job placement works out) is an attractive model.

The SEU recognises that "The solution to concentrations of worklessness will be different in different places. Sometimes the answer will lie in a neighbourhood, but often the solution will need action across a city or region... housing, planning and regeneration by local authorities are also crucial."[42]

The problem of worklessness might benefit from a more innovative local solution. The Social Exclusion Unit has long stressed that "involving communities, not parachuting in solutions"[43] is essential in regeneration work.

The fact that each geographical concentration of worklessness has its own particular challenges and circumstances suggests a need for community ownership of services.

For example, research by the Joseph Rowntree Foundation into the coalfields demonstrated the need to tailor service provision to the area's historical and sociological situation.

> "The lesson from the coalfields is that places subject to restructuring need strong support from national government and EU programmes. This support needs to be formulated, implemented and managed to help local people use their own creativity and talents to play a role in the regeneration of their distinct places. Programmes for regeneration need to recognise the specific requirements of individual places."[44]

The prevalence of multiple needs – including health, education and housing needs – among workless people, show that joined up, user-focused solutions will be most effective.

The relatively centralised Jobcentre Plus model may not be the most appropriate means of facilitating innovation at a local level. In 2002, The Work and Pensions Committee highlighted the need for greater individual initiative from staff in responding to clients needs':

> "How much of the vision is about moving people towards work, and how much about providing a better service through a more integrated approach? How can the goal of a service tailored towards individual needs be met, within a regime driven by speed of throughput and job placement targets? These are difficult tensions to resolve and require

more individual initiative from staff in responding to the needs of a wide variety of clients; greater flexibility to adapt practice to suit local circumstance; new skills to engage with people at a distance from the labour market; and new tools to use to help them."[45]

The need for greater flexibility was acknowledged by the DWP in April 2003, through the creation of a new, annual £20 million discretionary fund (0.5% of Jobcentre Plus' operating costs), and more flexibility for Personal Advisers to allow early entry into the New Deal. The fund was combined with an incentives package for staff to improve performance, and additional budgets targeted at ethnic minorities.

Outlining the proposals, the then Secretary of State for Work and Pensions, Andrew Smith MP said:

> "This package will give local managers the flexibility and discretion to provide innovative, tailored solutions to local labour market problems, working with local employers to help more people move off benefit and into work."[46]

Commentators have drawn attention to the importance of social networks in lifting people out of disadvantage and worklessness.

> "There is no point in debating how to finance the future of welfare, unless we create a system of support for the poor and socially excluded which enables them to develop the kinds of social network they need."[47]

Third sector organisations, including the many housing associations which provide employment training, could be invited to work more closely with communities to improve the life chances of the workless. Closer community ownership of the Jobcentre Plus models, perhaps through franchising, would help to provide the workless with greater access to pre-existing networks. Depending on the particular needs facing individual workless people, other specialist third sector organisations, such as Shaw Trust, could be brought in to deliver tailored support.

**Employment training in Australia**

The present government in Australia has taken steps to outsource publicly funded employment training to the independent sectors.

Ten years ago, provision was shared between the public, private and third sectors in roughly equal proportions. Since then, the government has withdrawn from direct service provision. Its role is now restricted to commissioning and regulation, with
the private and third sectors each delivering about 50% of the services commissioned.

The two largest providers of employment training services in Australia are third sector organisations: the Salvation Army, with around 10% market share, and Mission Australia, with around 9%.

Mission Australia has grown fivefold since 1996, and now employs 3000 staff in 300 separate locations. A significant number of staff members have been transferred from public sector employment. Its employment services target disadvantaged job seekers, particularly those who have been unemployed continuously for more than 12 months.

Following a robust analysis of demand, organisations are incentivised to recruit clients, receiving 20% of their full fee on sign-up. The remainder is paid on a performance related basis. The Australian Government is currently consulting on steps to streamline administration and increase consistency across competing providers.[48]

Potential third sector contribution in expertise and added value

*Efficiency and impact*

There is strong independent evidence that the leading third sector organisations provide high-quality, customer focused services, closely tailored to hard to help clients. One reason for this may lie in their ability to provide joined-up services, working across the boundaries between central and local government, and between those distinct local governmental agencies.

An independent study of **Tomorrow's People** by Oxford Economic Forecasting identified the following hallmarks of Tomorrow's People's work:

- One-on-one contact with clients – A Tomorrow's People adviser will spend 45-60 minutes with a client per meeting, compared to the 14 minutes they would receive at Jobcentre Plus,
- An environment of trust – many clients come forward by word of mouth, recommended by friends and relatives who have already been helped and trust the organisation to deliver,
- Good links with employers – understanding their requirements and building up trust that applicants forwarded will be appropriate for their organisations,
- Focus on after-care – so that both the employer and employee know that if any problems arise in the early stages of their relationship they can call on Tomorrow's People for support,
- Independence from government – making it easier to win the trust of clients who may be wary of speaking to 'authority-figures'.

On average 76% of those helped by Tomorrow's People are in work 12 months later. There are also wider benefits which accrue to society as a result of improvements in the health of those who find jobs through Tomorrow's People: a reduction in child poverty and social exclusion, and lower levels of crime.

In addition, economic benefits arise from the training assistance which Tomorrow's People has provided. Oxford Economic Forecasting has calculated that these economic benefits are worth around £450 million. For every £100 invested by Tomorrow's People, the whole of society is £160 better off in the long-term through lower expenditure, additional taxation receipts and wider economic and social benefits.

### Off the Streets and Into Work (OSW)

The OSW partnership works with a variety of people, from different backgrounds and with many diverse needs. The common thread is that they have been excluded from and found it difficult to access employment, or training, guidance and support from mainstream agencies.

- 63% of OSW clients are hostel residents, while 12% are recently resettled, and 7% are rough sleepers (58% have had experience of sleeping rough at some time).
- The large majority (90%) of the people OSW supports are unemployed, and 21% of clients have been unemployed for more than 3 years.
- 57% of OSW's clients do have relevant work experience and 47% have relevant qualifications. 20% of clients have identified literacy needs and 16% have identified ESOL needs (i.e. English is not their first language).
- 22% of OSW clients have one or more extra support needs relating to alcohol, drugs or mental health issues.
- 14% of clients are refugees or asylum seekers.
- In the period April 2003 – March 2004 OSW worked with 2,145 clients, 1,232 of whom had come to OSW for the first time.
- 254 clients achieved an accredited qualification, or credits towards a qualification.
- 347 OSW clients progressed onto further education or training.
- 255 clients progressed on to other services or specialist support.
- 230 clients went into employment (42% of jobs were permanent and full-time).

The Chief Executive of **Shaw Trust**, Ian Charlesworth, has said:

"The services we provide to the public sector are better value for money than those provided by the state, are delivered to more clients and achieve better employment outcomes than public sector alternatives.

A supported workshop in Middlesborough illustrates our success. Under the Local Authority the workshop was losing £750,000 per annum, but is now breaking even under our management. When the workshop is fully transferred to us we confidently predict it will be in profit within two years, offer more jobs to disabled people and provide more job opportunities for people to transfer to other employers on increased rates of pay. These are all outcomes that are seen as desirable by the purchasing authority."

There is no reason, in principle, why Jobcentre Plus' objective could not also be delivered by third parties, under contract to the government. By encouraging independent providers to take them on, in addition to training objectives, government would ensure that users receive a joined-up service.

### Driving change

A group of 16 independent employment providers, spanning private and voluntary sectors, and receiving total government funding of about £300 million, recently commissioned Oxford Economic Forecasting to draft a position paper on the issues they face. The main barriers to an expansion through contestability lay in poor procurement practice, and closely resemble the issues identified in Surer Funding.

---

"A step-change in the culture of procurement is required if the government is to achieve the best outcomes for the employment providers' sector and for the people they help. To achieve this positive change the government should work with industry to:

- help raise **awareness** of best procurement practice across government departments,
- ensure that relevant government recommendations are implemented in full and without delay through regular **auditing** of previous and existing contracts and by **enforcing** these principles in future contracts,
- encourage a **partnership** approach to delivery, namely a funder-contractor relationship characterised by trust and the mutual objective of getting as many people from target groups back into employment,
- develop a **"kitemark"** for funders who pass certain basic standards, as recently proposed by acevo.

Changing the culture in which business is conducted can improve operational efficiency, by reducing costs and increasing outcomes, bringing mutual benefits to both government and employment providers alike. Without addressing these issues the government is unlikely to fully exploit the benefits from contested service provision."[49]

---

Through the newly formed Employment Related Services Association ERSA, 12 independent providers have united with the aim of agreeing policy positions on procurement best practice. While in many areas the providers will continue to compete, they recognise that collective negotiation over the contractual framework will enable all to achieve better results.

In advancing this agenda, we propose a model to involve third sector organisations more strategically in employment services, encouraging citizens and communities to become more actively involved in tackling the problems of worklessness. The components of our model are:

1 Franchising individual Jobcentre Plus offices to pathfinder consortia, combining community ownership with specialist providers, to tackle worklessness in areas where it is most concentrated. As about a third of housing association tenants are unemployed or workless, housing associations would be natural partners in this alliance.

2 Exploring the possibility for further joint ventures between public, private, and voluntary sectors, encouraging government to share the risks and rewards contingent on success in delivery on a long-term basis.

3 Improvement and standardisation of Jobcentre Plus' procurement relationships with providers that specialise in reaching the hard to help.

# Chapter 4: Children's services

## The market segment

Plans have been recently announced to provide childcare facilities to all working parents of school-age children. This will be done in part through the establishment of Children's Centres in every ward across the UK by 2010, building on the Sure Start programme and other initiatives.

Children's Centres will contribute towards the Government's commitments to:

- the best start in life for every child,
- better opportunities for parents,
- affordable, good quality childcare,
- stronger and safer communities.

The core offerings of Children's Centres focus on:

- childcare and early education,
- health,
- family support and advice,
- employment services.

Schools are intended to provide a similar offering from 8am-6pm for children of school age and their parents, as part of the Extended Schools programme.

Although there are real challenges in coordinating a coherent and viable third sector offering, this area has the potential for a large-scale third sector involvement in shaping, coordinating, commissioning and delivery key services. There is a danger that, without clear action, this opportunity will be missed.

Policy and budget responsibility

Lead policy and budget responsibility for the childcare initiatives lies with the Department for Education and Skills (DfES), under the leadership of Rt Hon. Beverley Hughes MP, the Minister for Children, Young People and Families.

The DWP is another major stakeholder, under its Public Service Agreement (PSA) target "to reduce the proportion of children in workless households by 6.5% from 2003-2006", and its joint PSA target with HM Treasury to "reduce the number of children in low-income households by at least a quarter by 2004". These contribute to a broader target of halving child poverty by 2010 and eradicating it by 2020.

DfES is the main source of central funding for Sure Start, within three streams:

• The Nursery Education Grant funds a free part-time place for all three- and four-year-olds in early years education.
• The Early Years and Childcare Grant is the main grant for local authorities to develop the National Childcare Strategy.
• Funding is available for disadvantaged areas, Children's Centres, special educational needs, training and quality, and childcare development.

Local education authorities have a duty to secure a free, part-time early years education place for every four-year-old for the three terms before they are of compulsory school age. The Nursery Education Grant forms part of the local authorities' statutory funding settlement. Private and voluntary organisations can also apply, provided that Ofsted assesses their services as being satisfactory.

Scale/value of segment

The last of the 524 Sure Start Local Programmes was approved in December 2003, and they are now all up and running. There are currently 192 Children's Centres. The service is expected to reach 650,000 children by March 2006. The Government has announced that there will be 3,500 such centres by 2010.

According to the DfES, the Government has created 920,000 new childcare places since 1997, benefiting over 1.6 million children.[50]

Informed by the childcare review, the 2002 Spending Review settlement unveiled:

- a combined £1.5 billion budget for Sure Start, early years education and childcare, including more than doubling childcare spending, by 2006,
- the establishment of a network of Children's Centres for up to 650,000 children and their families,
- the creation of a further 250,000 new childcare places - in Children's Centres and elsewhere - by 2006, on top of the existing 2004 target of creating new places for 1.6 million children.[51]

2003 spending on Sure Start totalled £900 million. The 2004 Budget announced £669 million additional funding for Sure Start by 2007-8 compared with 2004-5, an annual growth rate of 17.3%.

### Current provision and the third sector's role

Local authorities have been given strategic responsibility for the delivery of Children's Centres. They are planning the location and development of centres to meet targets set by the Sure Start Unit, in consultation with parents and other key partners. They are now responsible for delivering initiatives such as Sure Start local programmes, Early Excellence Centres, the Neighbourhood Nursery Initiative, and Children's Centres.

Since the funding for children's services are not ringfenced, there is some concern amongst commentators that not all of it will reach the desired frontline services. In particular, preventative services may be considered less important.

The natural destinations of the funding are children's trusts, newly created models within local authorities, intended to bring together all services for children, and young people within an area, providing a focus on improving outcomes. An announcement of 35 successful Pathfinder Children's Trusts was made jointly by Margaret Hodge MP, then the Minister responsible, and Stephen Ladyman MP in July 2003. The Government expects all areas to have a Children's Trust by 2008.

**Children's Trusts: new ways of working**
"What Local Authorities are required to have in place by 2008 are the arrangements that produce integrated working at all levels, from planning through to delivery, with a focus on improving outcomes.

LAs may not choose to call this a 'children's trust' but the important point is that the way of working is in place and committed to."[52]

As a result of government funding, all local education authorities are now able to offer a free early education place to all three-year-olds in their area. Funding is made available at the rate of £416 a term. Providers must provide five sessions of nursery education each week for 11 weeks a term. Each session must be at least 2.5 hours long.[53]

Local authorities are encouraged to work with key local partners, although there is no explicit requirement to involve the third sector. However, the DfES has stated that "Local Authorities are expected to involve voluntary and community organisations at all levels of Children's Trusts – from governance to integrated service delivery."[54] A recent consultation paper shows a strong policy commitment to improving statutory relationships with the third sector.[55] Experts believe that the third sector is likely to be involved to some extent in all current partnerships, although this will vary widely between Early Years Development and Childcare Partnerships (EYDCPs).

Since local authorities have the lead responsibility for delivery, the likelihood is that many will prefer to provide services in-house rather than trusting the third sector to deliver them. It is significant, however, that 90% of nurseries are currently provided independently. Most are run by the private sector rather than the voluntary sector.

The third sector does lead and coordinate activity within some flagship Children's Centres.

## The Coram Community Campus: an integrated third sector Children's Centre

Coram Family is a leading children's charity that aims to develop and promote best practice in the care of vulnerable children and their families.

Thought to be England's oldest children's charity, it continues a tradition of public service delivery stretching back to 1739, when Thomas Coram established a Foundling Hospital to provide care for abandoned children living and dying on the streets of London.

It shares a three acre site in Kings Cross, London, with various Camden Council and NHS services, and several other charities. Collectively, they provide a unique multi-agency facility used by parents and children every day of the week in one of the UK's most deprived inner-city areas, comprising:

- nursery education and day care throughout the year for children aged six months to five years,
- after school care and holiday play schemes,
- services for children with special needs ,
- drop in centre and outreach work in the community,
- education, support and training for parents,
- specialist advice and support for homeless families and teenage parents,
- health and social work services,
- a child minders network,
- music therapy,
- community arts activities.

The core services are provided by the Thomas Coram Centre for children and parents. The Thomas Coram Centre was designated an Early Excellence Centre in 1998, and became one of the first Children's Centres in 2003.

Other services on the Campus are provided by:

**Camden Primary Care Trust** - providing a child psychology service.
**Collingham Gardens Nursery** - a parent-managed day care and education centre for 2-5 year olds.
**Field Lane Homeless Families Centre** - providing practical help and support for homeless families, refugees and asylum seekers.

**KIDS London** - providing services for children with special needs, including home-based learning, respite care and family support.
**King's Cross Homelessness Project** - providing advice and outreach to families living in temporary accommodation.
**TreeHouse Trust** - an educational centre of excellence for children with severe autism.[56]

Devolution and community ownership
The crucial need for community involvement and ownership in children's services provides the strongest argument for third sector involvement. Sure Start, for example, places a strong emphasis on community ownership. Experience in other countries highlights the importance of involving parents, in particular.

**Childcare in Sweden: parent cooperatives**
Swedish childcare aims to support and encourage children's development and learning, while enabling parents to combine parenthood with employment or studies.

During 2001–2003 reforms were introduced to improve access. The aim of these reforms was to make public childcare a part of the general welfare system, available to all. The basic principle is that all children in Sweden shall have access to childcare and that fees shall be so low that no child is excluded.

Local authorities were required to provide pre-school or family daycare openings to all children aged 1–5, even when the parents were unemployed or on parental leave. Free pre-school care was introduced for all children aged 4–5 during the school term. The government also capped the amount parents were required to pay for public childcare.

Local authorities provide grants for childcare by independent organisations. The size of the grant corresponds to the cost of equivalent statutory provision, and the fees charged may not exceed those charged by the local authority. In 2003 about 17% of pre-school provision was independent. The most common form of non-municipal undertaking is the parent cooperative.[57]

Illustrative examples given below suggest that some of the best practice in securing community involvement is found in the third sector.

**Sure Start Nuneaton: A Children's Centre Development led by NCH**

Sure Start Nuneaton was approved in July 2000, and covers a culturally diverse urban area within Warwickshire. NCH is the Lead Agency and the Accountable Body is North Warwickshire PCT.

Services operate from the Main building – Riversley Park Centre (owned by the PCT), an outreach venue (a refurbished shop), a local school, and a church building.

The team is made up of staff employed by NCH directly (Programme Management, Admin, Parental Involvement and Family Support) and those seconded in from partner agencies, but who receive operational management through NCH (Finance Manager, Health Visitor, Midwife, Speech and Language Therapist, Psychologist, Psychiatric Nurse).

The Centre provides:

- Early Education and Day care,
- Family Support and outreach to parents,
- Child and Family Health Services.

It also links with Jobcentre Plus, through a service level agreement. Jobcentre Plus sessions are held at Riversley Park every month, and CV writing courses are delivered as part of an adult learning programme.

The Programme Director, Julia Doyle, cites the following factors as key to its success:

1  a common understanding and commitment to integrated working and inclusive services through a child and family-centred approach,

2  developing and sustaining effective partnerships between agencies,

3  having a system in place for listening to children and families and responding where possible,

4  challenging inequity and poor quality provision, and

5  not compromising on quality.

Children's Centres in Folkestone and Margate, partly funded
by the state, are exploring forms of mutual incorporation to
involve key stakeholders in their membership and governance.
The standard company legal form, a Company Limited by
Guarantee, fails to promote community ownership.
Mutualisation of individual service providers may be a key
component of the Government's programme to devolve
control over certain public services down to a community level.
As Ed Mayo, Chief Executive of the National Consumer
Council, has put it:

"A co-operative or mutual structure which puts the interests of
the community at the top of the agenda has clear advantages.
A society where such organisations played a bigger part, with
greater opportunities for citizenship and the engagement of people
in their local communities, would be a more healthy society."[58]

For example, the Sure Start Folkestone Partnership Board seeks
to give parents a form of ownership and an ability to influence
the organisation's strategic planning. It comprises:

- 5 representatives elected by the local membership,
- 4 from other key local organisations,
- 3 from statutory health trusts,
- 2 from the local authority,
- the head teacher of the local school which houses the
  partnership, and
- 1 staff member.

It can be argued that some children's services are best delivered at a national level. For example, a parenting helpline
might best be provided by a partnership of national charities
focusing on children and parents. The insistence of Sure Start
on local ownership has led some to question the extent to
which local partnerships are duplicating effort. The local
nature of decision- making provides a disincentive for third
sector organisations to develop national consortia.

Opportunities for a greater third sector role
Third sector delivery brings considerable advantages to
children's services:

- An emphasis on community ownership encourages parental involvement, increasing the responsiveness of service delivery, and promoting more active citizenship.
- Independent organisations are regarded by many service users as less judgmental than statutory equivalents. Their separation from the state encourages a "hard to reach" service users to come forward.
- Third sector services may also carry less of a stigma than local authority services, encouraging a broader cross-section of the public to benefit from them.

Many observers believe that the third sector could take on a much more significant role in delivering children's services, in areas such as childcare, preventative health and social care. However, the major children's charities have expressed concern that the role of the third sector risks being neglected and marginalized.

---

**Third sector role: mainstream or margins?**

"Over the last ten years the sector's role as a provider of children's services has significantly grown through the contracting out of services by local government, especially of children's social services. Central government schemes such as the Children's Fund and Sure Start have also fuelled this growth, as well as giving large organisations like NCH new experience of leading these area-based programmes and of capacity building and commissioning services from small organisations."

"The government continually emphasises the enhanced role it wishes the voluntary sector to play in delivering public services, and schemes such as Futurebuilders and the Parenting Fund are designed to build our capacity to do so, with specific reference to provision for children, young people and families."

"We believe the paper wholly underestimates the role of the voluntary sector in running effective children's services and in improving children's outcomes. We are worried its proposals may also inadvertently marginalise us in the future."

(From NCH 2005, full response to Every Child Matters)

Within this market segment, particular areas seem highly suited to an increased third sector role.

### 1) Children's Centres

As outlined above, in a small minority of children's centres, the third sector has a leading role as a coordinator and provider of key services. The strengths of these case studies, particularly in promoting community ownership and supporting high quality services, suggest that the model should be rolled out across other areas.

The larger charities, some of which have been extensively involved in the delivery of Sure Start, are very well positioned to deliver services such as childcare within children's centres. For example, NCH already runs over 230 early years and family support projects across the UK, most based in areas of significant deprivation.

In addition, the third sector could take on a major role in the employment services that Children's Centres will deliver.[59] A partnership approach, combining national expertise with community ownership might secure the greatest "added value" from third sector delivery. As a matter of good practice, national charities seek to maximize the involvement of parents and community organisations in the centres they run.

The success of such a roll out would depend heavily on the availability and stability of targeted statutory funding, and the local capacity of third sector organisations to support it.

*As part of its strategy for children, the Government intends to support schools in offering services from 8am-6pm during term.*

## 2) Children's residential placements, and other specialist services

Each year about 60,000 children are separated from their families of which 20,000 are in residential care; the remainder are in foster care.[60] Although local authorities seek to provide this care as close to home as is possible, there is a dearth in provision. As a result, many local authorities now commission placements far outside their catchment areas.

Larger third sector organisations have a highly developed perspective on the needs of these children, and are motivated by the long-term goal of achieving ideal provision, rather than the more pragmatic issues of immediate local affordability. Their thinking focuses more on tightly on outcomes, making them potentially a key partner in any strategic review of provision.

Government could seek to involve the third sector more closely in the commissioning processes and standards, perhaps through a long-term think tank, with a view to improving long-term provision. Such an approach would also encourage the major children's charities to pool resources.

It is increasingly clear that specialized, low-demand services are no longer viable for individual local authorities and primary care trusts. There is scope for exploring regional and sub-regional models of delivery, which might closely involve the major third sector organisations. In particular, services for children with severe or multiple special needs might benefit from such an approach.

## 3) Extended schools

As part of its strategy for children, the Government intends to support schools in offering services from 8am-6pm during term. Such services are intended to play a similar role to Children's Centres, but for families with school-age children.

### The Extended Schools Pilot

In the 2002-3 school year, the Department for Education and Skills (DfES) sponsored twenty five local education authorities (LEAs) to develop extended schools pathfinder projects. Each project was free to determine the focus of its work, though

particular encouragement was offered to initiatives that would
lead to:

- schools that are open to pupils, families and the wider
  community during and beyond the school day, before and
  after school hours, at weekends and during school holidays,
- activities aimed particularly at vulnerable groups, in areas
  of deprivation and/or where services are limited,
- the promotion of community cohesion by building links
  between schools and the wider community,
- the provision of services to communities,
- a contribution to neighbourhood renewal, and
- a positive effect on educational standards.

While funding is channelled to participating schools through
LEAs, third sector organisations could play a significant role
in providing appropriate services, such as opportunities for
volunteering.

### Barriers to a greater role

The extent to which an expansion of third sector activity can be
successfully coordinated depends on three key factors:

(a) willingness within government to transfer responsibility
to the third sector,

(b) the capacity of the third sector to deliver high quality
services,

(c) the ability of the third sector to provide a coordinated
offering, ensuring Value for Money (VFM) with public
funds.

### (a) Willingness to transfer responsibility
### to the third sector

The formal responsibility to provide statutory levels of childcare resides with the social services departments of local authorities. Under the present arrangements, individual local authorities will only contract with the third sector if they have sufficient trust and confidence in the local sector's ability to deliver.
Many specialised third sector services are not viable if only

delivered at a local level. Without efforts to coordinate a regional or sub-regional approach to commissioning, localisation might provide a brake on the sector's ability to expand its role.

### (b) The capacity of the third sector to deliver high quality services

The infrastructure of the third sector remains relatively weak, compromising the confidence of both providers and commissioners to enter into large scale partnerships. The 2002-03 workforce survey showed that lower qualified and lower paid staff are concentrated in private and voluntary sector provision. In these settings, pay rates are relatively low, staff turnover is higher and providers often face recruitment difficulties.[61] These problems are often the result of the fractured and limited funding the third sector experiences.

### (c) The ability of the third sector to provide a coordinated offering, ensuring Value for Money (VFM) with public funds

Third sector organisations, including community organisations, have widely varying priorities. Some wish to deliver services, while others seek involvement in their planning and commissioning. Services are often far more specialised than the general offerings that individual local authorities are likely to prioritise. By offering government a more complete package, the sector achieves economies of scale and the government achieves efficiency savings through less contract negotiation with different suppliers.

Driving change

The emphasis of Children's Centres' proposals on responsiveness, service quality and community ownership makes them a natural candidate for the ODPM's "Sustainable Communities" agenda. The DfES aims to devolve decisions about local service delivery to local levels wherever possible, but as yet has no specific aims for community ownership through the third sector. In advancing this agenda, we propose a new model to place parents and third sector organisations at the heart of childcare services. The components of this model are:

1) Encouraging local authorities to act as procurers and coordinators of services, while leaving provision to third sector organisations, through a requirement that services are contested by specialist and/or community based organisations, and a target for levels of independent delivery.

2) Building delivery capacity through longer-term funding, which facilitates access to capital, and investment in third sector consortia, which enables third sector organisations to provide a more coordinated and higher quality offering in the high potential areas we have identified, such as Children's Centres and residential placements.

We recommend two further initiatives to support the model's success:

3) developing the sector's infrastructure to create a more coordinated voice, and

4) improving the funding relationship between local authorities and their third sector partners.

## Developing the sector's infrastructure to create a more coordinated voice

Investing in the third sector's specialist infrastructure on a long-term basis would help it to develop a more coordinated voice. This would lead to more successful partnership working with the more highly developed public and private sectors, which are strongly represented by the Sure Start Unit and the Private Day Nurseries Association respectively.

A better developed infrastructure might promote more ambitious models of third sector involvement in children's services and Children's Centres, building on the example of Coram Family, the Folkestone Partnership, and others. The DfES intends to take on some of this role, by collecting information on third sector involvement and sharing examples of good practice.[62]

From April 2006, The Government plans to invest £1 million to build the local third sector's infrastructure and capacity, followed by £2 million the following year. This constitutes 0.1-0.2% of the almost £1 billion annual spend on Sure Start. Some local areas, such as Kent, have created local infrastructure charities to support the local third sector. Others, such as Brighton and Hove, are bringing all local providers together into a consortium.

### Improving the funding relationship between local authorities and their third sector partners

Intervening to stabilise funding relationships between local third sector providers and local authorities would lead to higher quality, more reliable, and better value services delivered by the third sector. In turn, this would promote greater confidence and trust in the sector among local authorities and primary care trusts.

The Government has pledged to ensure that independent providers receive the funding they need to increase early education provision from 33 weeks per year to 38. The DfES is also consulting on "draft statutory guidance on local cooperation arrangements that makes clear its expectation that voluntary and community organisations are effectively engaged in all aspects of children's trusts".[63]

Alternatively, the success of such involvement could be measured as part of local authorities' Comprehensive Performance Assessments. The DfES also intends to publish guidance on commissioning, and to involve the third sector in its development.[64]

# Chapter 5:
# Independent living aids

## The market segment

The term "independent living aids" or "community equipment" encompasses the full range of specialist equipment available to disabled people, elderly people, and those with long-term medical conditions or disabilities living at home.

Examples of such equipment include:

- sensory aids, e.g. hearing aids, white walking sticks, reading stands,
- mobility aids, e.g. wheelchairs, rails and Zimmer frames, etc,
- other equipment, e.g. pressure care mattresses, commodes, bathmats, etc.

Such equipment is vital in promoting quality of life, independence and access to services. For a person with mobility problems, having a wheelchair or walking frame can mean the difference between leading a comfortable life and being a prisoner in the home. Independent living aids can be vital in ensuring a dignified standard of living for people who have either a temporary or permanent disability or illness.

Policy and budget responsibility
The budget for independent living aids is devolved to local level. Responsibility is split between primary care trusts, which take responsibility for sensory and health equipment, and local authorities, which deal with other independent living aids.

The policy lead is now with ICES (Integrating Community Equipment Services), a Department of Health

funded initiative across health and social care to remove
unnecessary barriers and promote the modernisation of services.

Scale/value of segment

Community equipment services (CES) provide the gateway to
the independence, dignity and self-esteem of some 4 million
older or disabled people and for 1.7 million informal carers.[65]
Audit Commission figures show that over £400 million was
spent on equipment in 2000. This is likely to have increased
substantially over the past five years, due to the attention
given to this area since then.

Impact and efficiency of current provision

In March 2000, the Audit Commission published *Fully
Equipped*, a report on the provision of some forms of equipment to older or disabled people by the NHS and social services
in England and Wales. Alan Milburn MP, then Secretary of
State for Health, recognised the report as "a very stark picture
of frankly a second-rate service in some parts of the country."[66]
It pointed to variations in all aspects of service provision, unrelated to underlying levels of need, and found that the quality of
services mainly derived from custom and practice, rather than
from any strategic overview of the contribution they could make.

Eligibility criteria are set locally, and vary according to the
budget available, meaning that provision does not always reflect
need. Recycling of aids varies between 20% and 70% depending
on the local authority. Coordinated and integrated delivery was
hampered by silos in both needs assessment and provision.

---

**Fully Equipped: The picture in 2000**

"*Fully Equipped* showed that the organisation of equipment
services was a recipe for confusion, inequality and inefficiency.
It found that many equipment services were small and fragmented, characterised by a lack of clinical leadership and senior
management involvement, and that they were failing to meet
the demands of clinical governance. Users did not always get
equipment of a reasonable quality meaning that some of the
money spent was wasted.

> The Commission called for urgent action to improve standards, provide a fairer service and make equipment services an important component of strategies designed to promote independence."[67]

Following the Commission's report, the Department of Health (DH) published a series of milestones for the delivery of integrated community equipment services by April 2004. The overall objective is to increase the number of service users by 50%. By 2006, an additional £1 billion will be invested in social care services for older people, tied to reforms. The measures include:

- expanded provision – half a million more pieces of community equipment benefiting an estimated 250,000 people,
- delivery in seven working days of community equipment (aids and minor adaptations), and fines for delayed delivery,
- faster assessment – by the end of 2004, first contact by social services will be made within 48 hours and the assessment completed within one month, with 70% of assessments completed within two weeks, and
- increased choices for older people – following assessment of care needs, all councils will be obliged to offer direct payments to all older people allowing them to make their own decisions about the secondary care they need.

Potential third sector contribution in expertise and added value
The Red Cross loans over 2,000 lines of community equipment all over the country. In some areas, it also assesses users' needs. It has particular expertise in the coordination of complex logistical models, vital in ensuring the delivery of equipment to high standards of services.

*the Red Cross staff in the Leicester service handles 7,500 calls per month and delivers almost all equipment within seven working days*

**The British Red Cross: Community Equipment in Leicestershire**

The British Red Cross is the largest third sector provider of community equipment in the UK, helping tens of thousands of people in need each year. For the past nine years the British Red Cross Community Equipment Services in Leicester has held the contract with the local council and health services to manage all community equipment services for Leicestershire and Rutland, helping over 20,000 people per year. More recently the Red Cross has won similar contracts to manage CES support for Barnet and Doncaster.

Run from a small call centre and a warehouse in the centre of Leicester, the Red Cross staff in the Leicester service handles 7,500 calls per month and delivers almost all equipment within seven working days.

As a bulk-buyer of community equipment, the Red Cross is able to secure favourable terms for equipment purchase. The equipment remains the property of the funders (which gives them more flexibility when it comes to renewing contracts) and the Red Cross charges a nominal fee to the relevant councils for each item delivered or collected. Last year, 70% of the equipment issued was from recycled stock and all items are bar-coded with an audit trail showing service history and usage.

The Audit Commission has officially cited Leicester as an example of good practice. Other statutory authorities seeking advice on how best to operate such a service regularly visit the Leicester BRC CES site, which continues to expand its service year on year. In 2004, the Leicester service won a national Department of Health award for innovative use of IT.

Although many community equipment services are achieving greater integration, relatively few have tackled the difficult issues surrounding the provision of equipment for people with sensory disabilities as well as physical needs. In such cases, assessment is often duplicated and disjointed, services are unresponsive and variable in quality, and procurement is inefficient.[68]

A consortium comprising the Red Cross, RNIB and RNID was formed in April 2004, and has now been awarded a Department of health contract to establish a virtual community equipment store. Through the virtual store, public sector agencies are able to purchase items of community equipment from each other.

There is scope to develop still further the third sector's capacity to deliver high-quality, user-centred community equipment services in partnership with the state. A dynamic partnership between the Red Cross and the major charities tackling sensory disability would have the potential to make radical improvements to community equipment delivery, meeting NHS and Social Care Modernisation targets.

The consortium could build on the success of RNID in transforming audiology provision, harnessing the purchasing power of the state to drive up the quality of the equipment used. At present, local authorities purchase the equipment separately, resulting in equipment that falls well below the standards evident in the USA and Europe.

Contractual relationships between statutory agencies and providers suffer from the four key problems identified by Surer Funding:

- excessively short-term commitments,
- undervaluation and low pricing,
- counterproductive levels of uncertainty and risk placed on providers, and
- waste through excessive bureaucracy.

A joined-up approach to procurement would deliver major efficiency savings, freeing resources to invest in higher quality, more appropriate provision. A model of shared purchasing would closely reflect one agenda outlined by the Gershon Review in 2004.

---

**Efficiency through shared procurement: the Gershon agenda**

The Review team concluded that in general significant scope exists for delivering procurement savings, in particular through the further professionalisation of the procurement function within the public sector through either use of shared procurement models, or the enhancement of procurement skills.[69]

The RNIB and RNID have highly developed expertise in visual and hearing aids. Disability charities, such as John Grooms and Leonard Cheshire, have corresponding knowledge of the needs of disabled people. Together they could provide sufficient expertise in complementary areas to reform the full range of community equipment provision.

### Driving change

At present the third sector organisations within the consortium lack the capacity for a major national roll out independent living aid provision. We propose the following model to generate extra capacity, placing users at the centre of independent living aid provision:

1) The development of local pathfinder programmes, bringing the third sector consortium together with local authorities and primary care trusts, and piloting national commissioning guidelines.

2) The establishment of a new Community Interest Company, owned by major charities, to build the capacity for a national roll-out of provision. This should draw on the experience of the RNID in its national programme of audiology reform.

3) The integrated equipment service, including the virtual store, should in the future be opened directly to the public, perhaps through a system of vouchers or direct payments. This would increase user responsiveness and provide an element of user choice.

# Chapter 6:
# Correctional services

## The market segment

### Policy and budget responsibility

The Home Office is responsible for the delivery of correctional services. The 2004 Spending Review aims to ensure that "More offenders are caught, punished and stop offending, and victims are better supported." The Home Office holds the budget for both the Prison Service and the Probation Service, which are currently in the process of being brought together into the National Offender Management System (NOMS).

### Scale and value

A total of £3.5 billion will be spent on the delivery of custodial and community sentences in 2004-05, and plans for 2005-06 have been costed at £3.8 billion. This is divided between prisons and probation; two distinct areas of work with differing potentials for involvement of the third sector. Around 75,000 people are currently held in jails in England and Wales.

Crime currently costs the UK economy £50 billion a year (Audit Commission, 1998). It reduces business profits, imposes huge costs on the NHS, and widens inequalities in wealth and opportunity.

### Current third sector role

There is already significant third sector engagement with both the Prison Service and the Probation Service. There are over 900 different voluntary and community sector organisations already working in prisons delivering over 2,000 projects between them. More than 600 projects currently work with probation in the community."[70]

The probation service currently spends £40 million through the third sector on mental healthcare provision. This is mainly on drug and alcohol treatment, and on learning and skills.

## The case for change

### Impact and efficiency of current provision

The Carter review of correctional services, published by the Strategy Unit in 2003, indicated that far greater use is being made of them, although the number of people arrested and sentenced remains fairly constant.[71] It stated that additional investment in prison and probation has improved delivery:

> "The Prison Service has dramatically reduced the number of escapes, improved decency and increased the number of offenders achieving basic skills. The creation of the National Probation Service has given greater focus to performance management and seen the introduction of a range of new services."[72]

However, it also pointed to a number of failings including:

- resources have been concentrated on first time offenders, a poor use of additional investment,
- the system remains dominated by the need to manage the two services, rather than focusing on the offender and reducing re-offending.

Carter's recommendations led to the establishment of the National Offender Management Service (NOMS), with a single Chief Executive. Dealing with 225,000 offenders at any one time, NOMS will have a total workforce of approximately 70,000 people and a budget in excess of £4 billion. Central to NOMS are the principles of "end-to-end" offender management and of service integration, whereby offender managers take responsibility for planning all aspects of each offender's supervision.[73]

Leaders within the prison service have argued that conditions for prisoners fail to meet their needs, including their physical and mental health needs. The influx of mentally ill prisoners has increased dramatically over the last 15 years. 72% of male and 70% of female sentenced prisoners suffer from two or more mental health disorders; 14 and 35 times the level in the general population respectively.[74] Martin Narey, the NOMS Chief Executive, said in February 2005 that:

> "90% of those entering prison [in 2000] were recognised as displaying one or more forms of mental disorder - that is, alcohol addiction, drug addiction, psychosis, neurosis or personality disorder… The proportion of individuals com- ing into custody who show evidence of profound or medi- um psychosis has risen about sevenfold since the introduc- tion of care in the community."

He also said that conditions for 20% of inmates are "little short of gross", as they are sharing cells meant for only one person.[75] Moreover, the organisational culture within prisons has often focused more on punishment than rehabilitation. For example, Narey has described Wormwood Scrubs as a "deeply violent and evil place," and the staff culture at Wandsworth as "utterly reprehensible". Narey, suspended about 10% of Wormwood Scrubs staff for "brutality" and removed the governor of Brixton.

Prisons are, at present, particularly unlikely to provide a suitable culture for the rehabilitation of vulnerable young people. It is estimated that 80% of young people incarcerated in Young Offender's Institutions re-offend on release. More specifically, commentators have pointed to the failure of prisons to provide a safe environment for young girls:

> "Even if physically separated from the adults, girls held in prison are still living in a punitive adult culture with high levels of self-harm, suicide, poor staff training and low staff ratios. Prisons are simply no place for children".
>
> Frances Crook, Director, Howard League for Penal Reform

The disproportionate number of black people in prison present particular challenges for prison services. According to Home Office figures, in March 2003, 1% of black British adults were in prison. Black prisoners make up 16% of the prison population, but only 2% of the total population.

Recent studies suggest that racism is rife in prisons, and mechanisms to tackle it are not well used. One study of Young Offenders' Institutions reported that, "The vast majority of interviewees never made complaints through official procedures because they were unaware that official complaints procedures existed".[76]

Similar concerns have been raised over the culture in asylum Detention Centres. For example, in March 2005, following an undercover investigation into Oakington Immigration Reception Centre, 15 employees of the private provider Global Solutions Ltd were suspended from frontline duties.

The experience of Black and Minority Ethnic Voluntary Organisations in representing and working with their client groups will make them natural partners in shaping a response to these challenges.

A clear disconnect exists between many prisons and the wider community. In particular, commentators have argued that prisons are letting the public down through a failure to focus on re-offending rates. Given the huge cost of crime to the UK, initiatives on crime prevention can ultimately prove extremely cost effective.

Sir David Ramsbotham, former Chief Inspector of Prisons warned that a "bureaucratic overload" was holding prisons back in their efforts to stop inmates re-offending, by diverting the attention of governors from treatment and rehabilitation.

"Prisoners are people, not commodities, and must be treated as such," he said.[77]

In 2002, The House of Commons Home Affairs Select Committee recommended that "the Prison Service must take a longer term view of its duty to protect the public and devise targets which measure rates of re-offending".[78] In response, The Home Office's Spending Review 2002 set out a target to reduce re-offending by 5%, as measured by reductions in reconviction rates. A new target was outlined in the 2004

Strategic Plan to reduce re-offending rates by 5% by 2007-2008, and by 10% by the end of the decade.

Restorative justice attempts to bridge the gap between offenders and communities, by bringing offenders and victims of crime together with a view to making amends. The third sector is in a favourable position to deliver restorative justice services, particularly mediation work with offenders, victims and the community, as third sector organisations are seen as neutral by all parties. Restorative justice:

• sees the harm done by crime an offence as against a person or organisation,
• allows victims the opportunity to participate,
• brings victims and offenders together with an impartial facilitator to consider from all points of view what has happened and find out what can be attempted to help put it right, and
• encourages responsibility and reintegration.[79]

---

**The Prison Fellowship: restorative justice in action**
The Prison Fellowship is a registered charity that trains some 2,000 volunteers from all Christian denominations to support prison chaplains. Support is given to all who request it, regardless of their beliefs.

The Sycamore Tree Programme is a victim awareness programme that uses restorative justice principles. The content is covered in six sessions designed to enable prisoners to understand the impact of their crime on victims, families and the community.

It also encourages prisoners to accept personal responsibility for their actions and points to the need to make amends. Surrogate victims come into prison to tell their stories. At the end of the programme, prisoners are given the opportunity to take part in symbolic acts of restitution, taking the first step towards making amends for their past behaviour.

An independent evaluation by Sheffield Hallam University showed widespread and significant improvements in prisoners' empathy with victims, considered by NOMS to be a key factor in reducing re-offending rates.

By allowing the best prison governors greater freedoms, government might make more progress in its attempts to reduce re-offending. In place of the "bureaucratic overload" referred to by Sir David Ramsbotham, more independent prisons could foster a mission-driven, community-owned culture of innovation. Reconstituting prisons as not-for-profit organisations, with closer links to their communities through trusteeship, would provide one means of effecting this change.

### Potential third sector contribution in expertise and added value

To ensure cost effectiveness and foster innovation, the Government is keen to encourage competition in the provision of correctional services. It believes that opening up the 'corrections market' will allow many more organisations to use their skills and expertise to bear in helping offenders to turn away from crime. The Government expects to see partnerships developing that harness the respective strengths of public, private and third sector agencies.

Helpfully, as the services restructure to create NOMS, third sector engagement has significant profile as an issue on which research effort has been focused. This stems partly from recommendations in the Carter report:

> "The benefits of competition – from the private and voluntary sector – could be extended further, across both prison and probation. The introduction of competition in prisons has provided a strong incentive for improvements in public sector prisons."[80]

NOMS has identified the following advantages from their current partnerships with third sector organisations for the delivery of services:

- "a client centred approach and an emphasis on user involvement in their service provision,
- increased trust from offenders due to their independence from the public sector,
- the use of volunteers which allows services to increase social contact and, in both prisons and community-based services, provides an important link to local communities,

- continuity for prisoners returning to the community,
- a flexible, innovative and non-bureaucratic style – bringing fresh thinking to problem areas and new approaches with the advantage of being less risk averse and able to put ideas into action quickly."[81]

The scope for increased third sector engagement is much greater than is widely realised, both in the management of prisons and prison services, and in community-based services. Within each of the areas explored below, third sector organisations have a significant, if fragmented role. Their strengths could be harnessed far more effectively given a more stable framework within which to work.

Management of prisons

Prisons are already run by the private sector, along with similar institutions such as immigration detention centres. The ownership of the buildings either lies within a PPP or remains in the hands of the state, with only the management function transferred.

Prisons are recognised as failing in their objective of rehabilitation, so re-offending rates are currently being targeted for action. Specialist expertise for certain areas of rehabilitative work within prisons, such as counselling, education, and life skills, is already provided by the third sector.

---

**Third sector services in prisons**

The Samaritans are crucial in assisting suicide prevention in prisons and, through their training and support of prisoners as Listeners, bring the added benefit of providing an opportunity for positive engagement for prisoner volunteers.

Most visitor centres attached to prisons are run by voluntary groups who deploy volunteers from the local community, thereby not only offering an important service to prisoners' families, but also creating contact between the prison and its immediate community. "Time for Families" is an initiative in the Prison Service Eastern Area to promote greater awareness and more effective responses to the needs of children of prisoners. This is a unique collaboration between Prison Service, the Ormiston Children and Families Trust and the Lankelly Foundation.

Organisations also add value to learning and skills in prisons and in the community, by contributing to prisoners and offenders gaining accredited qualifications in basic and work skills, but also providing a means to engage learners who have had little contact with formal education. Arts organisations, for instance, offer a variety of routes to engagement through drama, music, dance, writing, story telling and visual media and opportunities for raising self-confidence and self-esteem. Youth workers offer an informal young person centred approach to engagement with young prisoners and juveniles. Parenting classes and family days offer support in maintaining relationships with partners and children and organisations that provide specific services to women prisoners help to meet their specific needs and offer practical and emotional support.[82]

Many acevo members working with prisons have expressed frustration at the apparent lack of coordination in their procurement processes. They point to prisons that work with many different voluntary sector providers, each delivering a similar service, without providing stable funding for any one of them. Liverpool Prison, for example, currently works with 91 separate voluntary organisations. In common with many other areas of third sector provision, providers have difficulty negotiating contracts that provide a stable and fully funded basis for service delivery, evaluation and development.

In recognition of this problem, the Prison Service has shown increasing willingness to improve its procurement and contracting processes. NOMS now aims to develop a new framework for commissioning.

**Risk sharing with the voluntary sector: HM Prison Service**
HM Prison Service employs a number of voluntary sector bodies to deliver services to offenders who are also drug users.

Reflecting concerns surrounding these contracts and growing experience of commissioning with the voluntary sector, the prison service has redesigned the contracts. These second-generation contracts are due for roll-out in 2005.

The Prison Service's approach to funding voluntary organisations is a pragmatic one. It appreciates that the voluntary sector is often uniquely placed to provide these services and stresses the importance of maintaining a strong and participative relationship with these organisations. At the same time there is a keen awareness that the need to meet targets requires that the funding relationship works.

**The funding relationship**
The Prison Service awards contracts for these services in all the prisons throughout the UK. In addition to a standard three-year minimum contract, each provider agrees a local 'establishment agreement' that is appropriate to their own circumstances and contains specific performance targets.

Unlike many of the instances we have discussed where the contractual relationship overwhelmingly loads risk onto the provider, the Prison Service takes a different approach.

Organisations are funded under a mechanism where contract revenue is linked to performance. The Prison Service provides an element of guaranteed funding to the provider: at the least, the contracts guarantee that revenue will be sufficient to meet employees' wages at the end of every month.

The mechanism of variable payment is designed such that only a portion of funding is put at risk and providers are not penalised for changes unrelated to their performance. For example, should services be undeliverable due to reasons such as an epidemic or a riot in a prison, providers are not penalised. The Prison Service understands that it is not in their interest to let providers incur significant financial damage.

This approach makes the effort to apportion risk sensibly and reasonably to the party best able to manage it. The approach is fundamentally about sharing risk. Risk is not loaded onto providers but is consciously balanced between purchaser and provider when agreeing the funding agreement. Appreciating the risks associated with service delivery is the first step towards a more efficient and effective engagement with the voluntary sector.[83]

The priority given to making rehabilitative work effective could be dramatically increased by giving third sector organisations a leadership role within prisons. Such a role could be generated by involving third sector organisations more directly in the strategic direction of prisons.

New forms of prison management or ownership would need to demonstrate their ability to maintain confidence in prison security. The third sector would either need to gain expertise in wider prison management or work together with public or private sector companies that can fulfil this role.

For many charities, direct involvement in prison management would be countercultural. While they recognise the clear need to improve standards of care in prisons, the scale of the challenge involved encourages caution. Kathy Evans, the Children's Society's Policy Director, says:

> "Unless children's welfare is the primary focus of decision-making and of the care they receive it is dubious as to whether we could, just by our philosophy, bring the humane approach they are seeking out. The humane approach should be built in all the way through."[84]

However, an increasing number of third sector organisations are taking on bolder correctional ventures, working in partnership with the public and private sector. In 2004, the Milton Keynes Secure Training Centre opened. CfBT, a major third sector provider of educational services, is providing education and life skills training for young offenders within the institution, which is managed by a commercial company.

Several other major third sector organisations are currently in active discussions with the private sector over potential joint ventures in prison management. The efforts required to bring together these partnerships might be rewarded by innovative joint ventures that blend the commercial skills of the private sector with the more user-focused culture of third sector organisations.

In entering new partnership arrangements with private companies, third sector organisations must retain their close focus on the welfare of prisoners and their independence to challenge the status quo. To ensure that prisoners receive the full benefit of greater third sector involvement, commissioners and providers avoid delivery contracts that constrain organisations in identifying and criticising poor practice or standards.

Delivery of justice (including custodial and community sentences) currently commands a total resource budget of £2.5 billion in 2004/2005. Capital investment into the prison service was £265 million over the same year. The transfer of assets would enable significant funds to be raised for investment by organisations which would otherwise lack substantial resources. Complications would undoubtedly arise if the properties themselves were transferred away from central government, although local asset transfer has enabled the independent social housing sector to flourish.

Pilot projects could focus on prisons where rehabilitation, rather than maximum security, is the priority. In this context, prisons need strong links with their local communities, making third sector involvement very beneficial. Key sub-sectors would include open prisons, and prisons for young offenders, in which many third sector organisations are already active.

---

**Mentoring prisoners: The Trailblazers Programme**
Trailblazers is a mentoring programme based inside HMYOI Feltham, providing Mentors to young male offenders in custody. Mentees are linked to a Volunteer Mentor from the community for approximately one year. Visits take place inside the prison every 2 weeks during the last 6 months of a prisoner's sentence then continue for a further 6 months post-release to help ease the transition back into society.

The selection process for mentees is minimal: any prisoner who wishes to join the programme can do so.

In addition Trailblazers also offers a life skills programme for prisoners. Topics include careers advice, job search skills, interview techniques, drug and alcohol awareness and making choices, which all help prepare for their release.

210 young offenders have benefited from mentoring via Trailblazers. Of those, only 17% have re-offended so far. Home Office statistics show that 76% of Young Offenders re-offend within 2 years of leaving custody. In comparison out of the 210 Trailblazer mentees, 55 have been released for over 2 years and only 31% have re-offended.

---

Work in prisons

Evidence shows that having a job on release is a key factor in reducing re-offending. The Home Office found that released prisoners were less than half as likely to re-offend if they were helped to find and keep a job. Prisoners themselves cite finding a job, alongside a home and a stable relationship as the three most important factors in preventing them from re-offending.

A Social Exclusion Unit report in 2002 found that most prisoners have never experienced regular or high quality employment, with more than two thirds of prisoners unemployed in the four weeks prior to imprisonment (compared to 5% of the general population). Three quarters of prisoners do not have paid jobs to go to on release. At present there is no obligation on prisons to provide care, employment or housing to those who have been released. There is a clear disconnection between correctional services and the wider community.

There is also little evidence that prison work in its present form improves prisoners' chances of finding employment, or their ability to lead law-abiding lives in the community. Reasons cited for this failure by the Howard League for Penal Reform include:

• work in prisons is menial, usually involving repetitive and low skilled tasks,
• the work available does little to reinforce the work ethic or provide the broader aspects of gainful employment such as social status, social interaction, career progression, long-term financial reward or involvement in workplace development,
• the nature of prison work is usually unlike that on the outside – machinery and processes are outdated, 'interruptions' reduce productivity and prisoners are usually 'passive' and uninvolved in the development of the products they produce,
• few prisoners are offered the opportunity to undertake integrated qualifications that relate to their work and are important in enhancing their future employability,
• because remuneration is so low, prisoners do not take part in the full earning experience including paying tax and NI, or learning about savings or budgeting to support their family.[85]

Third sector organisations are taking on a growing role in

increasing the life chances of prisoners. Some already work in partnership with prisons and other third sector organisations to establish employment opportunities on a social enterprise model. However, this is not yet seen as a core service by prison authorities. Rather, it is considered an optional, if desirable, addition.

---

**Inside Out Trust: employment skills for prisoners**

The Inside Out Trust develops prison projects based on restorative justice principles. The Trust works closely with prison staff and prisoners, and with a multitude of voluntary and community organisations, to set up projects which link the needs of charities and community organisations all over the world with people who live and work in prisons.

Prisoners learn new skills that they willingly use to provide goods and services to disadvantaged people all over the world; new skills that should improve their own employment prospects after release.

Each project:

- is a partnership between the Trust, a prison and at least one other organisation,
- gives prisoners the opportunity to gain transferable skills and, where possible, a recognised qualification,
- builds confidence, self-esteem and concern for the needs of other people,
- improves each prisoner's chance of gaining employment after release.[86]

---

*The third sector already has considerable involvement in correctional work in the community, with over 600 organisations delivering services. There is scope for a huge increase or even a complete transfer of delivery away from the state.*

> **The Design Studio**
> The Howard League for Penal Reform is setting up a social enterprise, The Design Studio, to provide real work for prisoners. They will be paid the minimum wage for the first time ever in the UK. They will have to start a bank account, a pension, save for their release and will be encouraged to donate towards Victim Support.
>
> This will enable them to take responsibility for their finances and their lives and prepare them for life in the community. As well as the opportunity to learn a trade and experience what doing a hard day's productive work means, prisoners will gain work related qualifications and a portfolio to help them gain a job on release.

### Community-based services

The third sector already has considerable involvement in correctional work in the community, with over 600 organisations delivering services. There is scope for a huge increase or even a complete transfer of delivery away from the state.

The National Probation Service (NPS) employs 18,000 staff. Its aims are to:

- minimise the impact of crime on communities and especially victims who have been touched by serious violent or sexually violent crimes,
- rehabilitate offenders given community sentences and those released from prison,
- enforce the conditions of offenders' court orders and release licences, and to protect the public.

The Probation Service has a good record of working successfully with the third sector to provide resettlement services to offenders in the community. Key areas of service delivery include:

- accommodation through hostels and "move on" housing,
- employment and housing advisory services, and
- drug treatment and rehabilitation services.

However, this work has been fragmented, with no coherent framework to build effective collaborations. Although the National Probation Service sought, after 2001, to develop a national strategic framework for its partnerships, work was overtaken by corporate changes, given lower priority than other initiatives, and, to some extent, superseded by the creation of NOMS. [87]

Commentators acknowledge that to meet obligations of accountability, a statutory probation officer will always be necessary to coordinate, supervise, and commission probation services. However, many believe that third sector service delivery would achieve better results than statutory equivalents.

The following characteristics of third sector organisations would bring particular benefits to probation work:

- increased trust from offenders due to their independence from the state,
- community ownership, providing a solid foundation for probation work through links between prisons and communities,
- expertise in rehabilitation, employment, and housing combined with a clear focus on outcomes and results,
- expertise in managing volunteers from diverse backgrounds, with a view to developing their skills and citizenship.

---

**Training prisoners as advisors: case study**

The 12ftx7ft cell at Brixton prison in south London might normally house two men, two beds and a toilet. But this one has a desk and chairs, and approval has been granted for a phone line.

Corbin Thomas and Richard Summer survey their office. Both long-term prisoners, they are also employees of the homelessness charity, St Giles Trust, and are two of Brixton's first six prisoner peer advisers offering support for their fellow inmates on housing issues.

Up to 60% of prisoners are homeless on release, according to the trust, and half lose their housing while serving their sentence. The charity believes that working to save tenancies or to find new accommodation will help cut re-offending rates.

The scheme started two years ago at Wandsworth prison, London, and the charity now recruits prisoners in seven jails in the south-east to offer housing advice and support. All are given training to NVQ level 3 in Advice and Guidance and so far 35 have qualified, with a further 26 currently studying for the certificate.

David Bailey, who gained the Advice and Guidance NVQ while he was in HMP Bullingdon, is now employed in the outside world by St Giles. His job is to liase with prisons involved in the scheme. "Let's face it, inmates open up more with each other," he says. "The prisoners are the best people for the job."[88]

**BTCV: volunteering and diversity**
According to BTCV, only 1% of staff in environmental voluntary organisations are from an ethnic minority. While 7 out of 10 black Britons regard looking after their local environment as 'very important', they are much less likely to be involved in community work than whites.

The environmental volunteering charity (BTCV) is determined to do something about this. It has already succeeded in increasing the proportion of staff from BME groups among its own workforce from 3% to 5%. It is also striving to include asylum seekers, refugees, immigrants and travellers in its volunteering work. But it has even more ambitious horizons.

The charity wants staff in its 200 offices across the country to reflect the diversity of the communities they represent, so that in mainly black areas, most staff should be black, and it thinks other environmental organisations should do the same.[89]

**Driving change**
A new consultation document, *The role of the voluntary and community sector in NOMS*, has recently been published. The document is an open invitation for strategies to increase third sector participation within the scope of NOMS. A new "Voluntary Sector Unit" has now been established within NOMs. Recent research[90] has highlighted the potential contribution of the sector and identified five barriers to an increased third sector role:

- cultural differences,
- capacity issues,
- structural problems,
- difficult funding regimes,
- unequal access.

As in many other areas of third sector engagement, there is a clear need to reform the funding regimes under which third sector providers currently operate. For example, the fragmented nature of arrangements between prisons and local third sector providers means that contracts are extremely difficult for either side to plan and manage effectively. They remain short-term, insecure, and undervalued, making them unfit for purpose in developing an effective, long-term, rehabilitation strategy for offenders.

In 2002 the Social Exclusion Unit commented, "The involvement of the voluntary sector in correctional work has been blighted by a lack of strategy, a lack of dedicated resource, a failure to capitalise on and continue innovative practice...and funding which is short-term, ad hoc and fragile".[91]

Under NOMS, ten new Regional Offender Managers will control much of the spending the system, with accountability to the National Offender Manager. This reform presents huge opportunities for third sector organisations to push for more stable funding, and to bid to roll out successful programs across regions. However, there is a real danger that smaller third sector providers will "fall through the gaps" in commissioning, not possessing sufficient capacity or expertise to bid for the larger contracts, which are likely to be let on a regional basis.

NOMS might seek to harness third sector expertise by commissioning services horizontally, funding specialist organisations to deliver tailored services across a region in partnership with the mainstream providers. This will create new opportunities for organisations to deliver services both inside and outside of prisons, ensuring greater continuity for offenders. Such models will make partnership working across the sectors increasingly crucial.

**Partners in Reducing Re-Offending**
Partners in Reducing Re-Offending (PiRR) is a one-year, cross-London project aimed at building effective partnerships between third sector organisations to reduce the levels of re-offending. It is one of six projects across England commissioned by the Voluntary Sector Unit (VCS) in NOMS to co-ordinate the skills and capacities of the VCS to deliver the reducing

re-offending priorities of the Regional Offender Managers. Revolving Doors Agency will lead the project in close partnership with a range of voluntary organisations and statutory agencies.

PiRR will provide an opportunity for London's third sector to prepare together for the new arrangements emerging out of NOMS. In particular, it will provide a practical forum for working through the significant challenges and opportunities of integrated commissioning and contestability and for negotiating the third sector's response.

In advancing this agenda, we propose two measures to transform the culture of correctional services, including community-based services, open prisons, and young offenders institutions. The aim would be to help offender services to meet their aspirations and targets on rehabilitation and crime prevention, through increased community ownership and engagement. Third sector organisations will be key partners in shaping and delivering the services that fulfil this aim. The two components of our model are:

1 Developing a more strategic and stable framework to drive up the levels of procurement of community-based rehabilitation services from the third sector, including

a) a requirement that such services should be contested by community-based organisations, and

b) an explicit commitment to the principles of acevo's Surer Funding Framework.

2 Exploring the possibility for joint ventures between public, private, and voluntary sectors to take on the management, and potentially even the ownership, through a stock transfer, of prisons. Pilot institutions should include open prisons, detention centres, and young offenders institutions.

# Chapter 7: Other areas of high potential

The four areas of service provision outlined above represent only illustrative examples of the third sector's potential. Many other areas of service provision also present major opportunities for a greater third sector role, to the benefit of service users. The areas briefly outlined in this chapter are not intended to be exhaustive, but each clearly deserves fuller exploration than has been possible in this publication.

### Mental health

Social inclusion has begun to assume a central role within the Government's programme for mental health services, as in many other areas of service provision. The Government has placed a correspondingly increased emphasis on the specialist strengths of third sector providers, particularly in increasing access to community resources, respecting individual needs and promoting user choice.

The Government's strategic aims in reforming mental health services include a greater role for the third sector in service delivery. A significant increase has already been brought about through the work of major third sector service providers. Third sector organisations such as Rethink, for example, already deliver an extensive range of community support services.

Some third sector organisations have begun to deliver mainstream services: Alternative Futures, for example, delivers services to hospital inpatients. The sector's strengths might lend themselves to a greater role in other mainstream areas, such as residential care and employment services.

Yet the third sector's current role falls far short of that

experienced in other countries. For example, the third sector's 30% market share in New Zealand compares with only around 5% in the UK.

The UK third sector's greatest challenge is to build the capacity required for a greater role in improving services for its beneficiaries. If one of the larger mental health trusts were to outsource even 20% of its current services to a single third sector provider, the organisation would become the largest in its field. Individual organisations recognise the need to collaborate in building the capacity to meet these challenges, and have established a Mental Health Providers Forum to guide this process.

---

**Platform: the umbrella body for mental health providers in New Zealand**

Platform exists to give voice to the non-government organisations (NGOs) that provide health and disability services in communities throughout New Zealand. It is an Incorporated Society funded by membership fees, philanthropy and fee for service contracts.

Platform members have a commitment to mental health and work collaboratively to find solutions that work for people and support New Zealand to provide leading edge mental health services.[92]

---

### Drugs

The Government's programme for drug treatment services is governed by a cross-governmental Public Service Agreement, which has a particular focus within the Home Office, the Department of Health, and the Department for Education and Skills. The priorities are to reduce the harm caused by drugs and drug related crime, including health costs and wider social and economic costs to society.

Drug Action Teams (DATs) are local partnerships charged with responsibility for delivering the National Drug Strategy at a local level, with representatives from the local authority: education, social services, housing, health, probation, the prison service and the third sector. Growing levels of third sector engagement reflect its contribution at community level in providing services for drug users.

Drug users with complex needs are a particular concern for third sector organisations. Although numbers are necessarily hard to gauge, organisations estimate that large numbers of people in desperate need of personalized services are, at present, failing to engage with provision. Turning Point has proposed three high-profile measures to expand and develop third sector provision to meet the complex needs of these users.

1) A **Voluntary Finance Initiative (VFI)** to allow not for profit organisations to play a fuller role in providing social care services. VFI would involve longer-term, more standardised contracts that voluntary agencies could borrow against to invest in capital or other development costs. The crucial difference between VFI and the existing Private Finance Initiative (PFI) is that all of the money raised would stay within the running of social care services rather than generating profits for a private company.

2) A **national detox chain**: a network of rapid-access residential treatment centres across the country. Based in each major city with a need, and drawing on Turning Point's Smithfield Service in Manchester, they would allow local residents to enter treatment at the point they most required it.

3) **Connected Care Centres** in every deprived estate in the country, providing all of the support services a community needs under one roof, literally taking social care to those who require it most. They would combine health, mental health, disability and substance misuse services with support and advice around benefits, education, housing and employment.

### Schools

The Government's manifesto for education in schools aims to maximize choice within a closely governed curricular and organisational framework. It recognises that:

"Britain has a positive tradition of independent providers within the state system, including church and other faith schools. Where new educational providers can help boost standards and opportunities in a locality we will welcome them into the state system, subject to parental demand, fair funding and fair admissions."[93]

Third sector organisations already contribute substantially to the education of some of our most disadvantaged children. They do so in special schools and, for example, in community projects for young people who are excluded from mainstream schooling.

There is clear potential for third sector organisations to play a greater role in school provision. At present, schools broadly fall into one of two categories: they are either independent and supported by fees charged to parents, or within the public sector and free at the point of delivery. However, two current trends within education policy are challenging the rigidity of this separation, and suggesting a greater role for third sector models of delivery.

First, the Government aims to increase the independence offered to schools within the statutory sector. The Manifesto pledges that "Successful schools and colleges will have the independence to take decisions about how to deploy resources and develop their provision." The degree of independence granted to Academies, and the guiding notions behind Foundation Schools, reflect this aim.

Second, the Government wishes schools to take on a greater role in delivering services to communities outside of the standard school day. In particular, the concept of extended schools suggests a greater role for the independent sectors. The Government envisages that state schools will deliver "full programmes of after-school activities" by "working in partnership with the private and voluntary sectors."[94]

The Government's aims to extend, diversify and improve the services delivered by schools could be given a dramatic boost through greater third sector involvement. Some third sector organisations are already active in schools provision. CfBT, for example, owns and manages St Andrew's School in Rochester, and Oakfield Preparatory School in Dulwich. Others, such as the United Learning Trust and ARK, are seeking financial backers to work with them in developing new academies.

Third sector providers have an explicit and permanent commitment to educational excellence, making them natural partners for Government in increasing personalisation and choice. The Government aims to enable successful schools "to expand their size and also their influence... by taking over less successful schools." The potential role of the third sector deserves further examination within an increasingly diverse and competitive area of public service provision.

### Social care for older people

Over the next five decades, the number of people over 65 is expected to rise by over 80%: from 9.3 million to 16.8 million. The number of people over 85 will almost quadruple: from 1.1 million to 4 million.[95] Of the £14.4 billion invested in social care in 2004/05, £10.6 billion was spent on services for adults. While future improvements in general health make future demand difficult to gauge, it is likely that an increased emphasis will need to be placed on social care for older people.

The Government wants to give older people "greater choice over their care," through individually held budgets that bring together funding for a range of services, including social care and housing support.[96] Second, it wants to place greater focus on preventative services: well-targeted, early interventions that prevent or defer the need for more costly intensive support.

Third, the Government wants to develop joined-up services around the needs of individuals, making them easier for service users to access and manage. It wants to ensure that the first contact between with the statutory or voluntary sector leads an older person to all the services they require. As the Social Exclusion Unit comments:

"Clearly, joined-up services are desirable for people of all ages and from all backgrounds. Joined-up services are even more important for excluded older people, who may have limited additional contact with mainstream service providers and lack the confidence and social capital to seek out the services that they need."[97]

Meeting these challenges will demand a far higher degree of

service planning and integration than has yet been achieved. It will require a national approach and strategy, backed by sufficient funding to ensure action. Third sector providers have particular expertise in joining-up services around individual users. Most of them, however, specialise in a particular user group, geographical area, or both. Replicating this user-focus nationally, and across all patient groups, represents an exciting challenge for the two sectors in working together.

Providers will need to be proactive and coordinated in making older people aware of available services, without becoming intrusive. Some older people may need support in developing the financial literacy necessary to manage their budgets, and in using the new technology through which services will be most easily accessible. For example, the Government aims to ensure that every patient has an electronic NHS Care Record by 2010. Eventually, patients will have access to all their health information, enabling them to be more involved in making decisions about their own care and treatment. Meanwhile, Kent County Council is piloting an interactive self-assessment website for users of social care services.

The Government has begun to outline a commissioning framework for the third sector within this agenda. It recognises that "support for a strong and vibrant Voluntary and Community Sector is an essential component of our vision and developing the well-being agenda." Reflecting the principles of acevo's Surer Funding framework, the Department of Health aims to support full cost recovery, limit the bureaucracy involved in evaluation, and make sure that contract sizes and timescales enable third sector involvement.[98]

# Chapter 8: Barriers to change – an initial analysis

Despite widespread calls for greater involvement, the third sector remains a relatively small, specialised provider. Its income from government, at £3.7 billion, represents only 1% of total public spending. While many policy initiatives from government departments suggest a central role for the third sector, in most areas this has not translated into practice on the ground.

While data on the size and scale of the sector is incomplete, it is evident that its role in public service delivery remains relatively insignificant. In 2001, the third sector's income from government, including social housing, stood at only £3.7 billion. Although this sum excludes the significant assets gained by the third sector through housing association stock transfer, it stands at only 0.7% of total public spending.[99] In comparison, it is estimated that government spends nearly £100 billion per each year on goods and services from the private sector.[100]

Government figures indicate that spending on the third sector is actually decreasing as a proportion of total expenditure, suggesting huge potential for expansion. To ensure that an expansion of third sector activity is possible and desirable, both government and the third sector will need to pay close attention to a number of significant barriers.

## Procurement and finance

At the root of many of the barriers to change lies the simple fact that contracts for service delivery between government and the third sector are not yet fit for purpose. The vast majority of arrangements are short-term, highly insecure, undervalued and excessively bureaucratic.

Acevo's recent publication, *Surer Funding*, underpinned by research from New Philanthropy Capital, illustrated how all parties currently lose out through poor contractual arrangements:

- third sector organisations find it difficult to recruit and retain staff, to access and manage finance, especially capital, and to improve services,
- citizens receive services that are not as reliable, or high quality, as they could and should be,
- Government bodies achieve poor value for taxpayers' money in commissioning services.

The insecurity of relationships with government makes it especially difficult for the third sector to access start-up funding for new services. Trustees of smaller charities are often unwilling to take on the risks, both financial and reputational, inherent in public service delivery. More awareness of the sources of start-up funding already available would encourage a greater third sector role in delivery by providing charities with the means to militate against these risks. Such a move would help to encourage third sector organisations to adopt a more entrepreneurial mindset.

At present, both government and the third sector expend a huge amount of time and resource in managing short-term renegotiations of relatively small quantities of money. By placing funding on a more stable, performance-related footing, government would free resources for greater investment to the frontline, producing better services for users and better value for taxpayers.

These problems have been widely acknowledged by both sides. In 2002 the Treasury recognised serious concerns about the funding relationship, and called for reforms to include:

> "ensuring that the cost of contracts for services reflects the full cost of delivery – including any relevant part of the overhead costs...[and] moving to a more stable funding relationship – longer contracts and longer term partnerships."[101]

Such shortcomings in funding and procurement process are by no means unique to the UK.[102] A definitive study of the third sector in Canada demonstrated the prevalence of similar issues for the Canadian Third Sector:

| Issue | Reported Severity of Problem (%) | | | |
|---|---|---|---|---|
| | Small | Moderate | Serious | A problem |
| Reductions in government funding | 9 | 20 | 36 | **65** |
| Unwillingness of funders to fund core operations | 11 | 22 | 27 | **61** |
| Reporting requirements of funders | 16 | 19 | 8 | **43** |

Acevo has called for a "Surer Funding Framework" to enable more effective and efficient delivery by the sector. The four key principles are:

1 sharing the responsibility for risk,
2 fair costing and pricing,
3 cutting waste caused by bureaucracy, and
4 issuing contracts of an appropriate timescale.

The Surer Funding principles were reiterated last year in the Efficiency Review conducted by Sir Peter Gershon.[102] He called on government to "improves its funding relationship with the Voluntary and Community Sector by:

• improving stability by moving to longer-term, multi-year funding arrangements where possible,
• considering carefully the appropriate assignment of risk between the statutory body and the voluntary and community organisation when contracting for service provision,
• making further progress towards full acceptance of the principle of full cost recovery, ensuring publicly-funded services are not subsidised by charitable donations or volunteers, and
• streamlining and rationalizing monitoring, regulatory and reporting requirements."

Significantly, none of these recommendations need apply exclusively to the third sector. They would increase the quality and efficiency of independent providers from the commercial sector, particularly that of small businesses, as well as the third sector. While considerable attention has been given to procurement relationships with the private sector, particularly within the field of health, government has only now begun to recognise the third sector's potential as a major provider. The development and adoption of effective, standardised practices would benefit all parties.

"In contracting with the voluntary and community sector government bodies should not cut them any special deals. They should simply act more efficiently and professionally, applying the discipline and rigour which is being brought to bear on dealings with the private sector."[104]

Yet strong commitments from central government to reform have had relatively little impact on the ground, and its vision of a third sector competing "on equal terms" has not yet been realised. A National Audit Office report, published in June 2005, noted the lack of progress in implementing central government recommendations.

The Home Office has recently closed a consultation on "Compact Plus", a bold set of new proposals to incentivise funding reform. They include several ideas from "Surer Funding": an independent champion to identify best practice, a kite-mark for funders who improve their practice, and the possibility of financial penalties for those who do not. Adopting and mainstreaming these proposals across local government will be crucial to the long-term sustainability of third sector service delivery.

### Capacity and staffing

Part of the difficulty in building effective procurement relationships lies in the sector's lack of capacity. In many ways the sector's huge diversity is one of its strengths, enabling highly specialised service offerings and facilitating healthy debate over policy positions.

Of the 200,000 registered charities, just 2,400 of them receive two thirds of the sector's income. The vast majority of third sector organisations are small, both in terms of turnover and professional staffing.[105] This places limitations on the sector's ability to work effectively with government, both in developing a coherent, large-scale offering and in successfully negotiating an effective contractual relationship.

Many third sector organisations lack the capacity to invest in strategic development and growth. This reflects historic failure to recoup the overhead costs necessary for such investment. Until all contracts between government and the third sector reflect the full costs of delivery, in accordance with central government policy, the deficit in capacity can only grow.

The sector needs to place a particular focus on developing its skills in contract negotiation. Acevo and NCVO have drawn particular attention to this deficit, informing the Government's investment strategy for the sector:

"Voluntary and community organisations need to recognise that the current relationship with government is the most favourable the sector has experienced. The sector needs to take advantage of this environment where possible. The sector's Financing Hub will play an important role in helping VCOs to do this, particularly by supporting the development of stronger skills in contract negotiation".[106]

It is clear that the sector is not investing sufficiently in training and development, particularly in the fields of leadership and management. Its deficit in professional development and skills is similarly acute. The sector currently spends as little as 0.8%-1.3% of its turnover on training and development. In comparison, the public sector spends 2.7% and private sector 3%. Even this low figure may be flattering, since the sector enjoys high levels of provision of goods in kind.

The SSDA estimates that the largest change in national demand for qualifications will be at the highest level (NVQ4+): with an additional requirement of over 2 million[107] this decade. These figures suggest that, in common with the rest of the economy, the scale of the sector's management and leadership deficit is likely to increase dramatically over the coming decade. A small number of highly focused initiatives to fill these gaps should be developed as a matter of urgency.

Acevo is championing the drive for a "modern, enterprising third sector", supporting its chief executives in personal and organisational development.

A modern, enterprising third sector organisation:
- demonstrates the highest standards of professionalism in working with clients, staff, volunteers, and all other stakeholders,
- is effective, efficient and responsible in generating and managing funding streams and fundraising activities, and
- is passionate about achieving change and delivering results on behalf of clients and members,
- has governance structures, systems and processes that are "fit for purpose", ensuring accountability while enabling effective decision-making,
- promotes accountability and transparency in all its communications with stakeholders and the general public.[108]

One objection frequently levelled at this agenda is that the third sector would use voluntary staff for core service provision, at the cost of lesser professionalism and greater unemployment. This objection is misguided: the sector already employs the full-time equivalent of 1.5 million professional staff. Like voluntary income, volunteers must not be used to subsidise the resources of the state. Additional resources should achieve genuine enhancements in services for beneficiaries, rather than a reduction of public funding costs of paid employment. For example, social care providers such as Leonard Cheshire use volunteers to deliver "value adding" services in addition to those funded by government, such as gardening and sports for their beneficiaries.

A greater third sector role might well involve the transfer of paid employees from the public to the voluntary sector. Under TUPE[109] regulations, the rights of those employees are transferred along with the business. Two implied risks arise. First, the third sector may develop a two-tier workforce. Parallels in the commercial sector have raised serious concerns, particularly from the unions. Even more drastically, the sector may find it difficult, under current funding regimes, to cover the costs of these benefits.

Workforce stability may also suffer, since third sector organisations can offer only very limited job security on the basis of annual contracts with government. In the most extreme cases, third sector organisations are forced to issue redundancy notices to their staff at the end of every financial year, only to rehire those staff when the contracts are finally renewed.

These concerns reinforce the point that a greater third sector role in service delivery cannot take place successfully under the current contracting regime. While organisations may absorb the short-term costs and risks of a two-tier workforce, the model will eventually prove unsustainable. A renewed commitment to longer-term contracts and full cost recovery must accompany any such expansion, ensuring that the third sector is able to recruit and retain a high-quality professional workforce.

## Governance and accountability

Concern that the sector is not immune from the general loss of confidence in corporate governance has led to a concerted drive to improve its accountability and transparency. Commentators have argued that the sector's present standards of governance owe more to history than to effectiveness.

Professor Bob Garratt writes, "The corporate governance of NGOs is a hot topic at present. I have worked with some of them on this very issue and have come away disappointed by their innate conservatism and short-sighted need to keep a firm grip on the levers of existing organisational power. The corporate governance values of accountability, probity and transparency are not yet well developed in many NGOs – but need to be if they are to maintain their own long-term reputations."[110]

There is a specific tension between the voluntary tradition of charitable governance, historically one of the hallmarks of the sector, and the increasing risks and scrutiny to which trustees are subject. The idea of trusteeship as a "gift of time" does not always sit well with the onerous responsibilities and standards charities are expected to achieve in their accountability to stakeholders, particularly in relation to the rising standards demanded of public service providers.

Government has noted a "general consensus that 'one size does not fit all' and that the diversity of the sector means that prescriptive solutions are not always the way forward."[111] Many chief executives are now reviewing their structures with the intention of striking an appropriate balance between competing demands.

The sector's major representative bodies, including acevo and the NCVO, are shortly to publish a code of good governance for the voluntary sector. Reflecting best practice within the third sector, and drawing on the role of codes in the commercial sector, the new document will set challenging governance standards for organisations while encouraging flexibility.

More attention must be given to ensuring the best form of accountability between third sector organisations and their statutory funders. Third sector organisations are already subject to regulation and monitoring by a huge variety of bodies. In a submission to the Efficiency Review, acevo noted that some major charities are subject to scrutiny from over thirty distinct regulators.

Yet a great deal of this scrutiny appears to be duplicated and often unrelated to organisational performance. Research into the "Tackling Drugs" initiative showed that third sector organisations were compiling demographic data for four separate government bodies on a monthly basis, at different times and in different formats.[112] Meanwhile, the impact of well-intentioned efforts to reduce unnecessary bureaucracy, such as the Government's "Lead Funder" initiative, is frequently dented by institutional inertia.

Many third sector organisations are fiercely protective of their independence, and wary of compromising it through greater accountability towards funders, especially government. The level of bureaucracy often inherent in such relationships acts as a further disincentive to greater collaboration. A change of mindset will be needed for these third sector organisations to take on a greater role in service delivery. However, such a change is unlikely while the barriers outlined in this chapter remain untackled.

### Costs and risks

Perhaps the third sector's area of greatest expertise lies in its ability to work with the hardest to help. This chimes closely with ODPM's commitment to use "the experiences of the bottom 10% as a litmus-test of reform across government."

The third sector has always prioritised the need to "focus on the disadvantaged and champion them as services are transformed across government."[113]

However, a re-energised commitment to the socially excluded brings the risk of considerable and unforeseen risks to the public purse. The experience of Leonard Cheshire in Hollow Lane[114] illustrates the potential benefits of risk-sharing in developing innovative services targeted at the most demanding clients. In that case the cost overruns were manageable and accepted by funders, but experience will vary between client groups.

There is strong evidence that the long-term financial benefits of third sector work outweigh the costs. The New Economics Foundation has undertaken significant work on Social Return on Investment (SRI), looking at the financial value of the social and economic returns achieved. A pilot study of four social enterprises showed an SRI of between 1.3:1 and 1.8:1.[115]

For some statutory bodies, embracing new risks with the aim of developing more flexible and innovative services will prove counter-cultural. Processes of accountability for public spending incentivise public bodies to minimise the risks they incur, ensuring that expenditure is as stable and predictable as possible.

A key challenge for both government and the third sector lies in analysing the long-term value of programmes aimed at the hardest to help. Only by developing a greater understanding of the benefits such services bring, and the risks that they reasonably involve, will individual agencies be able to commit to the increased investment and flexibility they demand.

### An implementation drive is necessary

The report recommends a step-change in thinking to catalyse an expanded third sector role in public service delivery. Implementing the manifesto proposals will require decisive political will and a strategic and co-ordinated drive from the centre. Piecemeal reform, based on the third sector's present marginal role in public services, will not deliver a significant change over the next five years.

We therefore propose a cross-governmental 'implementation

team' within the Cabinet Office to drive reform. Championed by a Minister and chaired by a third sector leader, it would include representatives from the key central government departments, from the third sector, and from major private sector contractors. Its major responsibilities would include:

- researching potential areas for third sector expansion, analysing the benefits of transfers and scoping a framework to effect them,
- exploring potential catalysts and models to drive greater delivery, including the three models proposed in this paper,
- analysing and tackling the cross-governmental barriers to further delivery, particularly in funding and procurement.

# Chapter 9: Conclusions

Third sector organisations could, and should, have a central role in the Government's current programme of public service reform. Many third sector organisations aim to identify and articulate the voice of under-represented citizens, particularly those who are currently excluded from mainstream public services.[116]

Additionally, in a variety of public service markets, third sector organisations have shown themselves to be innovative, committed and effective public service providers. Such organisations have the potential to realise the Government's ambition to deliver personalised public services "free to all, personal to each."

Yet third sector organisations are currently held back by a framework that promotes inefficiency, restricts capacity, and stifles innovation. Our case studies suggest that radical reforms to the way in which services are commissioned would allow third sector organisations to develop and disseminate a new breed of coherent, citizen-focused services, tailored to local situations and individual circumstances.

To build on this piece of work, with a view to implementing such reforms, we recommend the following actions:

1 The Government should undertake more detailed monitoring of third sector involvement in public service delivery. Current figures only illustrate levels of expenditure, which fail to reflect the full extent of service delivery undertaken by the sector. More accurate data would provide a far more reliable indicator of the success of government's policy initiatives in driving forward third sector involvement.

2 The Government should establish a cross-governmental implementation team, to include representation from

central and local government, economists and the major third sector service providers, to scope a framework for transfer in more detail and make recommendations to the Cabinet Office within 18 months. These recommendations should focus on:

- the benefits of asset transfer, and strategies to overcome the barriers such transfer would involve,
- the role of triple ventures between the public, private and third sectors, in improving contracting processes and outcomes, ways in which to increase the contestability of individual public service markets, removing artificial barriers to entry, and
- the potential for a new investment fund of significant scale to build capacity.

3 Within each of the market segments we have highlighted, three pieces of further work should be undertaken:

- analysis of the added value in third sector service delivery from a user perspective, building on the work of the National Consumer Council,
- exploration of the potential for significant asset transfer from the public sector to the third sector, reflecting the experience of the social housing sector, and
- encouraging the establishment of delivery consortia by major charities, following the example within the Community Equipment Sector, and building on the experience of the Futurebuilder's Fund.

4 Additional market segments should be explored in more detail, including:

- mental health and learning,
- education in schools,
- drug treatment, and
- social care and older people.

# Appendix 1: The international third sector – comparisons

Johns Hopkins' comparative project identifies two distinct models of welfare state: the "Nordic model" and the "European-style welfare partnership."

## The Nordic welfare state model

This model features:

- a relatively large third sector,
- a large volunteer base, on average 4.1% of the economically active population, but a small third sector paid workforce (2.3%),
- limited reliance placed on private philanthropy and third sector organisations to deliver basic social and human services,
- a stronger third sector focus on advocacy, professional organisations, sport and recreation.

## Fig: Nordic model income analysis

| Income Source | Proportion of overall resource | Proportion of overall resource including volunteers |
|---|---|---|
| From market | 59% | 35% |
| From government | 33% | 20% |
| From philanthropy | 45% | 27% |

## The European-style welfare partnership

This model features:
- a relatively large third sector, averaging 7.8% of the

economically active population and exceeding 10% in Belgium, Ireland and the Netherlands,

- a significant paid third sector workforce: 5.4% of the economically active population against an all-country average of 2.7%,
- substantial levels of public sector support: nearly 60% of civil society revenue in Austria, Belgium, France, Germany, Ireland, and the Netherlands,
- substantial third sector service delivery, particularly social welfare services such as education (25% of provision) social services (23%) and health (20%),
- strong religious organisations, especially the Catholic Church, able to persuade Governments to funnel social welfare protections extensively through third sector providers.

As a result, there is an extensive pattern of partnership between the state and the organised third sector:

- in Germany this is called "the principle of subsidiarity": the authorities are obliged to turn first to the "free welfare associations" to solve social problems,
- in the Netherlands, this is called "pillarisation": state support is provided to various independent "pillar" institutions. For instance, the state finances universal education through payments to non-profit schools, many of them with religious and ideological orientations,
- in France, the 1980s decentralisation policies led to a significant growth in third sector institutions, funded by local government and responsible for a variety of service delivery functions,
- Israel, also, has been influenced by this model.

**Fig: European model resource analysis**

| Income Source | Proportion of overall resource including volunteers | Proportion of overall resource |
| --- | --- | --- |
| From market | 35% | 28% |
| From government | 58% | 46% |
| From philanthropy | 34% | 27% |

## Fig: Individual countries: comparative data

| Country | Turnover | Funding from fees | Funding from government |
|---|---|---|---|
| UK | $100bn | 34% | 36% |
| | ($78bn excluding volunteers) | (44% ex vol.s) | (46% ex vol.s) |
| Australia | $24bn | 51% | 25% |
| | ($19bn ex vol.s) | (62% ex vol.s) | (31% ex vol.s) |

The sector has played a longstanding role in the delivery of
welfare services to the community. It provides a wide range
of services, including:

- the distribution of food and clothing,
- education,
- health,
- housing and accommodation,
- childcare,
- counselling,
- legal advice, and
- religious services.

Key service users include families, the aged, young people,
people on low incomes, the unemployed, the homeless, people
with disabilities, and people with mental health problems.

In 1999-2000, 51% of the $3.9bn spent on welfare services
was transferred to the third sector organisations (OECD 2003).

| | | | |
|---|---|---|---|
| Sweden (Nordic model) | $20bn | 31% | 14% |
| | ($10bn ex vol.s) | (62% ex vol.s) | (28% ex vol.s) |

Most of the third sector economy is based on self-finance,
including membership fees, service fees, voluntary collections,
and commercial activities.

Lotteries seem to be becoming increasingly important for
many NGOs. Members of these organisations contribute services
on a voluntary basis which are worth SEK 60-70 billion on an

annual basis. (Ministry of Public Administration, 1995)

| USA | $675bn | 47% | 25% |
|---|---|---|---|
| | ($566bn ex vol.s) | (56% ex vol.s) | (30% ex vol.s) |

"While it is difficult to get a precise reading of the levels and changes in commercial revenue earned by non-profits, it clear that interest in such income (governmental contracts included) has risen over the past two decades" (OECD 2003)

| Italy (European model) | $ 47bn | 50% | 30% |
|---|---|---|---|
| | ($36bn ex vol.s) | (60% ex vol.s) | (36 ex vol.s) |

Fees and charges are a dominant source of third sector revenue, outdistancing government support and philanthropy.

| Germany | $142bn | 21% | 42% |
|---|---|---|---|
| | ($94bn ex. vol.s) | (32% ex vol.s) | (64% ex. vol.s) |

| Japan | Expenditure $94 bn 3.4% GDP (1990) | | |
|---|---|---|---|
| | Subsector | Percentage of third sector expenditure (Yen billions) | Employment (FTE) |
| | Culture & recreation | 1.2 | 16,201 |
| | Education & research | 39.5 | 444,931 |
| | Health | 27.7 | 534,412 |
| | Social services | 13.8 | 279,625 |
| | Environment | 0.2 | 2,616 |
| | Development & housing | 0.3 | 4,418 |
| | Civil Society/advocacy | 0.9 | 11,773 |
| | Philanthropic | 0.1 | 1,946 |
| | International | 0.5 | 4,591 |
| | Business associations & unions | 11.4 | 90,416 |
| | Other | 4.5 | 49,299 |
| | Total | 100 | 1,440,228 |

# Appendix 2: Acknowledgments

The author would like to thank the following for their assistance in developing this paper. Particular thanks go to Ann Rossiter, Acting Director of SMF, Ed Mayo, CEO of the National Consumer Council, and to Stephen Bubb, CEO of acevo.

|  |  |  |
|---|---|---|
| David Hunter | Policy and Development Officer | acevo |
| Filippo Addarii | Head of International Programme | acevo |
| Stephen Bubb | CEO | acevo |
| Stuart Rigg | CEO | Advance Housing and Support Ltd |
| Neil Hunt | CEO | Alzheimer's Society |
| Julia Unwin | Author and Consultant | |
| Jeremy Crook | CEO | Black Training and Enterprise Group |
| Anthony Lawton | CEO | Centrepoint |
| Neil McIntosh | CEO | CfBT |
| David Harker | CEO | Citizens Advice |
| Cliff Mills | Partner | Cobbetts Solicitors |
| Phil Street | CEO | ContinYou |
| Nicola Winter | Media Officer | Coram Family |
| Stephen Burke | CEO | Counsel and Care |
| Roger Howard | CEO | Crime Concern |
| Martin Redman | Business Development Manager | GEO Group |
| Frances Crook | Director | Howard League for Penal Reform |
| Virginia Beardshaw | CEO | I CAN |
| Tim Moulds | Director | Inside Out Trust |
| Beth Breeze | Deputy CEO | Institute for Philanthropy |
| Nick Pearce | CEO | Institute for Public Policy Research |
| Mike Shaw | CEO | John Grooms |
| Bryan Dutton | CEO | Leonard Cheshire |
| Udeni Salmon | Head of Volunteer Support | Leonard Cheshire |
| Cynthia Hansen | | London School of Economics |

| Peter Cardy | CEO | Macmillan Cancer Relief |
|---|---|---|
| Patrick McClure | CEO | Mission Australia |
| Aaron Hendricksen | CEO | Mission Australia UK |
| Jackie Worrall | Director of Community and Criminal Justice | NACRO |
| Ian Vallender | Director of Policy and Information | National Council of Voluntary Child Care Organisations |
| Clare Tickell | CEO | NCH |
| Warren Hatter | Head of NLGN Research Unit | New Local Government Network |
| John Copps | Researcher | New Philanthropy Capital |
| Martin Brookes | Head of Research | New Philanthropy Capital |
| Steve Murphy | Regional Offender Manager, London | NOMS |
| Linda Butcher | CEO | Off the Streets and into Work |
| Kevin Belcher | CEO | Pecan |
| Rory Scanlan | | Policy Partnership |
| Jon Sibson | Partner | PricewaterhouseCoopers |
| Peter Walker | Executive Director | Prison Fellowship |
| Maeve Sherlock | CEO | Refugee Council |
| Cliff Prior | CEO | Rethink |
| Julian Corner | CEO | Revolving Doors Agency |
| John Low | CEO | RNID |
| Ian Charlesworth | CEO | Shaw Trust |
| Wilf Stevenson | Director | Smith Institute |
| Jacqueline Cassidy | Head of External Relations | Social Market Foundation |
| Lisa Harker | Chair | The Daycare Trust |
| Susanna Cheal | CEO | The Who Cares? Trust |
| Lisa Taylor | CEO | Trailblazers |
| Richard Kramer | Director of Policy | Turning Point |
| Su Sayer | CEO | United Response |
| Andreas D. Schulz | University of Giessen | |
| Gordon Diffey | CEO | Vista |
| Richard Bolsin | CEO | Workers' Educational Association |
| Keith Faulkner | Managing Director | Working Links |
| Lucy Watt | Public Affairs Manager | Working Links |
| Bernard Taylor | Director, Centre for Board Effectiveness | Henley Management College |
| Stephen Lee | Director, Centre for Voluntary Sector Management | Henley Management College |

# Appendix 3:
# About the author

Acevo (Association of Chief Executives of Voluntary Organisations) is the professional body representing charity and not-for-profit sector chief executives in England and Wales, with 2000 members. It has developed a leadership position within a fast moving and growing third sector.

Nick Aldridge is acevo's Director of Strategy and Communications. He manages acevo's professional development services, and its policy and communications strategies. He has led acevo's drive to become one of the most influential and respected third sector bodies in the UK.

Nick project managed acevo's "Surer Funding" Commission of Inquiry, working with the third sector and government to design more efficient and effective business models for service delivery through the not-for-profit sector. He has developed and championed acevo's policy on "Full Cost Recovery", fast becoming the definitive method for third sector organisations to cost their work.

He also led acevo's "Rethinking Governance", pressing for greater professionalism and a more enabling framework for governance in the not-for-profit sector, and was a member of the steering group that developed the sector's new code of governance.

Before joining acevo, Nick researched public policy at IBM and at Whitehall and Industry Group, having graduated from Cambridge University. His interests include music, particularly modern jazz and flamenco guitar, creative writing, and travel.

# Notes

**Executive Summary**

1   Third sector organisations are defined, as in HM Treasury's 2004 Discussion
    Document "Exploring the role of the third sector in public service delivery and reform",
    as those which:
*   operate on a not-for-profit basis,
*   are mission driven,
*   are not directly accountable to ministers,
*   and are considered to be outside the public sector by the National Audit Office.

**Chapter 1**

2   HM Treasury 2004, "2004 Spending Review - New Public Spending Plans 2005 -
    2008: Stability, security and opportunity for all: Investing for Britain's long-term
    future"
3   Conservative Party 2005, "Manifesto for Charities" and Liberal Democratic Party
    2004, "Innovation, Flexibility, Choice"
4   Gordon Brown, The Times 11th January 2001
5   See the analysis in Unwin & Molyneux, in Joseph Rowntree Foundation (Forthcoming)
    2005, *The voluntary sector delivering public services: transfer or transformation?*
6   Acevo 2003, Rethinking Governance, p.29
7   Chapter 4, Children's Services
8   Paxton and Pearce 2005, "The Voluntary Sector and the State"
9   NCVO 2005, "The reform of public services: the role of the voluntary sector", 18
10  cf HM Treasury 2004, "Exploring the role of the third sector in public service delivery
    and reform" and Bolton "Voluntary Sector Added Value: A discussion paper"
    (NCVO 2003).
11  Will Hutton and Stephen Bevan, "Pluralism in Public Service Delivery" in acevo 2003,
    Replacing the State?
12  However, the bureaucratic nature of contracting and monitoring relationships with
    the public sector can mitigate against this strength.
13  acevo 2004, Surer Funding
14  acevo 2004, Surer Funding
15  ODPM 2005, p.22
16  Unwin & Molyneux, in Joseph Rowntree Foundation (Forthcoming) 2005,
    "The voluntary sector delivering public services: Transfer or transformation?"
17  Social Exclusion Unit 2005, "Excluded Older People: Interim Report"
18  cf opinion polls conducted by NCVO and the think-tank nfpsynergy in 2003-4.
19  New Economics Foundation 2004, "Social Return on Investment: Valuing What
    Matters".
20  acevo 2004, Surer Funding
21  ODPM 2005, Sustainable Communities: People, Places and Prosperity, p.43

**Chapter 2**

22  Or Registered Social Landlords
23  ODPM 2005, Sustainable Communities: People, Places and Prosperity.
24  Pawson and Fancy for The Policy Press 2005, Maturing assets: The evolution
    of stock transfer housing associations
25  Acevo 2004, "Surer Funding"
26  Charity Commission 2005, "Delivering on public services -
    charity commission announces landmark decision" – Press release

27 From the Greenwich Leisure web site, http://www.gll.org
28 acevo's research for the Sir Peter Gershon's Efficiency Review in 2004 suggested that 93% of third sector organisations delivering public services do so on the basis of annual contracts.
29 A Welfare to Work initiative
30 Capgemini and Manpower
31 Labour Party 2005, "The Labour Party Manifesto 2005", and Office of Public Services Reform, 2005, http://www.cabinetoffice.gov.uk/opsr
32 cf Ormerod P., "Replacing the State" in acevo (2003), Replacing the State
33 Institute of Public Policy Research (IPPR), "Building Better Partnerships", London 2002, p.41.
34 acevo 2004, "Surer Funding: the acevo commission of inquiry report"

**Chapter 3**
35 BBC News, 16th May 2005, "Blunkett makes welfare reform vow"
36 Social Exclusion Unit 2004, Jobs and Enterprise in Deprived Areas
37 ib.
38 Ib, p.11
39 ODPM 2005, p. 41
40 Office for National Statistics 2004, Labour Force Survey
41 Finn and Zahno K. 2002, "Getting Jobs and Changing Lives: From Harlem to Harlesden"
42 Social Exclusion Unit 2004
43 SEU 1998, Bringing Britain Together, p.10
44 Joseph Rowntree Foundation 2000, Coalfields regeneration: dealing with the consequences of industrial decline
45 First report of the Work and Pensions Committee, 2002, para 89
46 DWP 2003, "Jobcentre Plus to spearhead drive for local jobsearch solutions"
47 6, P 1997, "Escaping Poverty: From safety nets to networks of opportunity"
48 Mission Australia 2004, "All in a Day's Work: Annual Report 2004"; Interview with Patrick McClure, CEO, Mission Australia, 24th May 2005.
49 OEF 2005, Employment Related Service Provision in the UK

**Chapter 4**
50 DfES, A Sure Start for Every Child
51 10 Downing Street 2005, Factsheet on the National Childcare Strategy
52 http://www.everychildmatters.gov.uk/childrens-trusts/model-faq/
53 Sure Start/Daycare Trust 2003, Directory of Funding for Early Years Education and Childcare
54 http://www.everychildmatters.gov.uk/voluntary-community-organisations/
55 DfES 2005, Every Child Matters: Working with voluntary and community organisations to deliver change for children and young people
56 http://www.coram.org.uk/cccampus.htm
57 Swedish Institute 2005, http://www.sweden.se/templates/cs/BasicFactsheet____4132.aspx
58 Ed Mayo and Cliff Mills, in Mayo and Moore (NEF, 2001), The Mutual State
59 cf Section 2.2 Above
60 Estimates from the Who Cares Trust
61 HM Treasury 2004, "Choice for parents, the best start for children: a ten year strategy for childcare", p.25
62 DfES 2004, "Every Child Matters: Change for Children", p.32
63 ib., p.29
64 ib., p.31

**Chapter 5**
65 http://www.icesdoh.org/guidelines.asp?id=1
66 Alan Milburn MP, quoted on BBC News (29 March, 2000), "Action ordered for disabled"
67 Audit Commission 2002, Fully Equipped Update
68 Virginia Beardshaw in acevo 2004, Surer Funding
69 Gershon 2004, "Releasing resources to the front line"

**Chapter 6**

70 Paul Goggins MP, Speech, November 22nd 2005
71 Strategy Unit 2003, "Managing Offenders, Reducing Crime"
72 ib.
73 Home Office 2005, National Offender Management Service: Working together to reduced reoffending
74 N Singleton, H Meltzer, R Gatward, J Coid and D Deasy, *Psychiatric Morbidity Among Prisoners in England and Wales*, ONS, 1998
75 Feb 7th 2005, Evidence given to the public inquiry into the murder of teenage prisoner, Zahid Mubarek, at Feltham Young Offenders Institution.
76 David Wilson, for the Children's Society 2003. "Playing the Game - Experiences of young black men in custody"
77 Sir David Ramsbotham 2001, Speech as reported by the BBC, HYPERLINK "http://news.bbc.co.uk/1/hi/uk/1397487.stm" http://news.bbc.co.uk/1/hi/uk/1397487.stm
78 Select Committee on Home Affairs, Fourth Report, 2000
79 Restorative Justice Consortium
80 Strategy Unit 2003, "Managing Offenders, Reducing Crime", p4
81 NOMS 2004, "Managing Offenders, Reducing Crime: The Role of the Voluntary and Community Sector in the National Offender Management Service", p4
82 Home Office 2005, "Managing Offenders, Reducing Crime: The Role of the Voluntary and Community Sector in the National Offender Management Service", para 2.8
83 From acevo 2004, Surer Funding, p.94
84 Community Care March 2004, Charities reject Labour proposal to involve them in running prisons
85 Howard League for Penal Reform 2005, "The reality of work in prison - an introduction" (http://www.howardleague.org/work/introduction.htm)
86 Inside Out Trust 2005, "Employment Inside and Out"
87 Home Office 2005, Managing Offenders, Reducing Crime: The Role of the Voluntary and Community Sector in the National Offender Management Service
88 Clara Penn for The Guardian, Wednesday March 2, 2005, "An inside job"
89 Third Sector, April 21 2004, "Newsmaker: The mould breaker - Tom Flood, Chief executive, BTCV"
90 Senior P 2004, "Enhancing the role of the VCS: A Case study of Yorkshire & Humber region"

**Chapter 7**

91 Social Exclusion Unit 2002, "Reducing re-offending by released prisoners"
92 From Platform 2005, www.platform.org.nz
93 Labour Party 2005, The Labour Party Manifesto 2005, p.37
94 ibid.
95 Government Actuary 2004, Quoted in Department of Health 2005, "Independence, Well-being and Choice", p.22
96 Labour Party 2005, Labour Party Manifesto 2005, p.72
97 Social Exclusion Unit 2005, "Excluded Older People: Interim Report", p.57
98 Department of Health 2005, "Independence, Well-being and Choice", p.68

**Chapter 8**

99 HM Treasury 2005. Figures given relate to "voluntary and community organisations", as defined by government.
100 John Williams, Director of Public Services at the CBI, 2005, 'Transforming Procurement in light of the efficiency review: a suppliers' perspective."
101 HM Treasury 2002, Cross Cutting Review – "The Role of the Voluntary and Community Sector in Service Delivery"
102 Statistics Canada 2004, "Cornerstones of Community: Highlights of the National Survey of Nonprofit and Voluntary Organisations", p48
103 Gershon 2004, "Releasing Resources to the Front Line: Independent Review of Public Sector Efficiency".
104 Sibson 2005, "Contestability and the Voluntary and Community Sector (VCS)"
105 This situation is by no means unique. In Canada, for example 1% of non-profit organisations account for 59% of total revenues. (Statistics Canada 2004, Cornerstones of Community: Highlights of the National Survey of Nonprofit

and Voluntary Organizations, 21)
106 NCVO 2005, "The Reform of Public Services: The Role of the Voluntary Sector", p.6
107 SSDA 2002, p.10
108 acevo 2005, "A Modern, Enterprising Third Sector: A Manifesto for the Third Sector's Leaders"
109 Transfer of Undertakings (Protection of Employment), introduced in 1981 and revised in 2003
110 Garratt 2003, "Thin on Top: why corporate governance matters"
111 Charity Commission, Home Office, Audit Commission 2003, "Looking Forward to Better Governance -Seminar Report"
112 acevo 2004, Submission to the Gershon Efficiency Review
113 ODPM 2005, Sustainable Communities: People, Places and Prosperity, p.43
114 Chapter 1
115 New Economics Foundation 2004, "Social Return on Investment: Valuing What Matters"


**Chapter 9**
116 Baring Foundation and acevo 2004, Speaking Truth to Power